PATIENCE
CARD GAMES

**Trevor Day
and The Diagram Group**

HarperCollins*Publishers*

HarperCollins*Publishers*
Westerhill Road, Glasgow G64 2QT

www.**fire**and**wate**r.com

First Published 2000

Reprint 10 9 8 7 6 5 4 3 2 1 0

© Diagram Visual Information Limited 2000

Front cover photographs: (main picture) Tony Stone
Images/Tamara Reynolds; (insets, top to bottom) Tony Stone
Images/James Harrington. Telegraph Colour Library/Nick
White, Tony Stone Images/Vera Storman

First published as *Gem Patience Card Games* 1996
Many thanks to Isabella Percy for testing the card games

ISBN 0 00 472445 3

Printed in Italy by Amadeus S.p.A.

Introduction

Patience games (in the USA called solitaire games) are card games to be played by one. They have a marvellous capacity both to soothe and challenge the mind of the player. *Collins Patience Card Games* contains 90 such games. Within the book are a wide range of patience games, from simple to complex, from traditional to novel. Some require a straightforward approach, and work by themselves; others are much more challenging, and require precision, forward-thinking, and not a little ingenuity on the part of the player.

Each game is described with step-by-step instructions, complemented by clear explanatory diagrams. A sample layout is given for each game. The games are arranged by chapter, according to whether they require one or two decks of cards, and whether the decks are ordinary or stripped. Within each chapter, the games are arranged in order of difficulty.

Patience is perhaps the ultimate game – one in which you are clearly competing against yourself and where the luck of the draw (as in life itself) can help or hinder you. Win or lose, you will be in good company.

Napoleon Bonaparte, Emperor of France, and Leo Tolstoy, author of *War and Peace*, were among the most ardent players of patience.

Created by the Diagram Group, this book is an attractive companion volume to the same team's *Collins Card Tricks* and *Collins Magic Tricks*.

Grading of games

●   Easy   ✖   Difficult

◆   Moderate   ▼   Very difficult

Contents

SECTION 2. GAMES USING A STRIPPED SINGLE DECK

SECTION 3. GAMES USING TWO DECKS

SECTION 4. GAMES USING TWO STRIPPED DECKS

General guidelines

Shuffling

The pack, or packs, are first shuffled. If the cards are used regularly for playing patience, then it is important to get the cards back out of order from the previous game. Overhand shuffling, or riffle shuffling, done thoroughly and honestly, will get the cards out of sequence. An alternative method is to place all the cards face down on the table and slide them around with a circular motion to mix them thoroughly. This can be repeated once or twice to ensure thorough mixing. Another method is to deal out the pack into piles of about ten cards. As far as possible, the dealing is done at random, with cards added to one pile, and then another, in a haphazard way, often changing direction. The piles are then picked up at random, combined, and the pack finally given an overhand shuffle.

The general pattern of play

Most (but not all) games of patience follow a recognized pattern. The cards are first shuffled. Then some or all of the cards are dealt out on the table in a specific arrangement, called the layout. The main aim of the game is then to release certain cards (usually aces) from the layout as foundation cards. On these are built the remainder of the pack in numerical order within their respective suits.

If all the cards are not dealt to the layout at the beginning of the game, those left in the hand of the player are dealt either singly or in packets. Depending on the specific rules of the game, the dealt card is placed either on a foundation pile, on exposed cards on the layout or onto a discard pile.

What distinguishes one game from another is the particular set of rules by which the shuffled pack is rearranged into an ordered one. If the pack is successfully rearranged in order, and in accordance with the rules of the game, then the game is said to have 'turned out' or 'come out'. The player has won. If the position becomes blocked, so that no more moves are possible, then the player has failed. One of the seductive features of most patience games is that they are designed to fail more often than win.

Choosing a game

Within this book, the games in each chapter are sequenced in order of difficulty, with easy ones at the beginning and harder ones towards the end.

Harder here refers to two things: how easy it is for the game to come out by chance alone *and/or* how important it is for the player to make the best choices in each turn of play. Some games, such as Canfield (p.96) and Klondike (p.115), rely largely on chance and yet will come out only about one time in every 20-30. The few choices during play are settled by intelligent guesswork. Other games, La Belle Lucie (p.61) and Poker Solitaire (p.82) for example, offer many more choices, and careful play is necessary if the game is to come out, even when the fall of cards is favourable.

There are many ways of classifying patience games, and a single game can share similarities with a diverse range of other games, so classification can lead to confusion rather than clarification.

In this book, similarities between games are mentioned where they will help the player

make choices about which game to play. For
example, if the person has been playing
King Albert (p.33), and would like a change,
they may choose a clock layout game such
as Grandfather's Clock (p.30), or one using
a square layout, as in Queen's Audience
(p.40). On the other hand, if they have been
playing a Bisley-style game such as Baker's
Dozen (p.14) and want to try a more
challenging game of the same type, such as
Bisley (p.48) itself, it is easy to track down
such a game by using cross-references or
reading through the introductions for harder
games later in the chapter. The introduction
to each game often indicates the type of
game and suggests how difficult it is to win,
and why.

Glossary

available A card is available when, under the rules, it is available for play.

bezique pack A deck of 64 cards formed by removing all 2s, 3s, 4s, 5s and 6s from two standard 52-card decks.

blocked A game that cannot be won, because the fall of play makes it impossible for any card to be played or any move to be made.

building Arranging cards on top of each other during play in the order prescribed by the particular game. Most often this is by suit or by colour in numerical order, upwards or downwards.

column Cards arranged vertically in a line.

coming out A game that achieves its aim and is totally resolved.

dealing Laying out the cards before play begins.

deck Pack or set of playing cards used for a game. Patience games are sometimes played with cards of smaller size than usual if space is at a premium.

discard To lay a card to one side, usually onto a discard pile, so that the card is temporarily out of play.

discard pile Cards are thrown face up on this pile when they cannot be used immediately to build. They can be brought back into play later, as appropriate.

exposed card Normally only face up, completely exposed cards are available for play. Cards partly covered are unavailable until fully exposed.

follow suit Building with a card of the same suit as the previous card on the pile.

foundations Base cards on which building takes place.

layout The arrangement in which the cards are dealt onto the table ready for play.

packet A given number of cards conforming to a particular requirement, e.g. a packet may be four cards of the same rank.

patience General name of card games for one player.

piquet deck A deck of 32 cards formed by removing all cards below the 7s from a standard 52-card deck, leaving the 7, 8, 9, 10, J, Q, K and ace of each suit.

rank Order of cards, or suits, in play. Higher ranks take precedence over lower ranks, e.g. 10 of clubs takes precedence over 9 of clubs.

redeal When the stock is exhausted, some games allow for redealing – the use of the discard pile as stock.

reserve Cards in the layout that are available for play but are not foundations.

row Cards arranged horizontally in a line.

solitaire Sometimes synonymous with patience but also the name of a board game in its own right.

spaces Gaps in the layout that may or may not be filled, according to the rules of the game.

stock Cards remaining face down in the hand when dealing is complete. They are used in play according to the rules of each game.

suits Clubs and spades are black suits; hearts and diamonds are red suits.

turning the corner A sequence in which the ace connects the top and bottom of the suits, e.g. Q, K, ace, 2, 3.

1. Single-deck games

◆ BAKER'S DOZEN

A classic game with simple rules, related to
Bisley (p.48). The game comes out more
often than not. It requires a moderately large
space.

Cards

One standard 52-card deck. If space is
limited, use small cards.

The layout

The entire pack is dealt face up in four rows

A sample layout

foundations

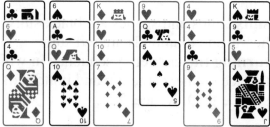

of 13 cards each, the four cards in each column overlapping. Aces, when released, go into a foundation row above the layout.

Aim

To build the suits in ascending rank order, from the ace to king.

Playing

● At the start, transfer every K to the bottom of its pile (see layout). Aces are placed in the foundation row as soon as they become available for play.

● The exposed card at the bottom of a column is available for play to foundations, building upwards within suit, or to play to other exposed cards, building downwards in rank order and regardless of colour or suit.

● Any spaces made by removing a whole pile may not be filled.

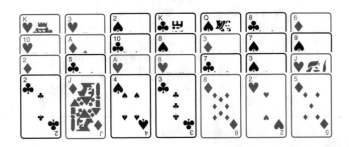

◆ BELEAGUERED CASTLE

A classic patience game, also known as
Laying Siege or Sham Battle.

Cards

A standard deck of 52 cards.

A sample layout

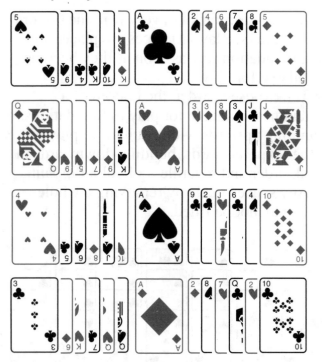

foundations

The layout

The four aces are placed face up in any
order in a central column. On the left of
each ace, deal one card, face up. Then deal
the same way to the right of each ace.
Continue dealing to the left and then right of
each ace, as before, but overlapping the
cards as they are dealt, until there are 'arms'
of six cards on either side of each ace.

Aim

To build on each foundation card a pile of
each suit in numerical order from ace to K.

Playing

● Any one of the eight exposed cards at the
outer ends of the arms may be selected for
play and placed either on the foundation pile
of the same suit to build upwards, or on the
end of any other arm to build numerically
downwards irrespective of suit.

● If an arm has no cards left, another end
card can be played into the space.

◆ CALCULATION

Also known as Broken Intervals, this game
requires thought and foresight.

Cards

One standard deck of 52 cards.

The layout

Choose any ace, 2, 3 and 4 and lay them in a
row at the top of the table as foundation
cards. Four discard piles are formed below
the foundation cards as the game progresses.

Aim

Disregarding suit, the aim is to build on
each foundation card in the following order:

On the ace, every card: ace, 2, 3, 4, 5, 6, 7,
8, 9, 10, J, Q, K.

On the 2, every second card: 2, 4, 6, 8, 10,
Q, ace, 3, 5, 7, 9, J, K.

On the 3, every third card: 3, 6, 9, Q, 2, 5, 8,
J, ace, 4, 7, 10, K.

On the 4, every fourth card: 4, 8, Q, 3, 7, J,
2, 6, 10, ace, 5, 9, K.

Playing

● One card at a time is turned up from the
stock and may be placed overlapping any of
the foundation cards, to begin building.

● If a card cannot be used to build, it may be

A sample layout

foundations

spaces for discard piles

A sample order of building

on ace	on 2	on 3	on 4

 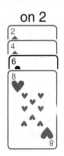  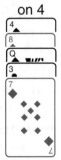

placed face up on any of the four discard
piles.

● As the game continues, the top card of any
discard pile may also be used to build, but
may not be transferred to another discard
pile.

● The skill lies in controlling the cards in the
discard piles. For example, Ks will be
required last so it will be helpful to keep
them either all in one pile or at the bottom of
each pile.

● Ideally, cards should be built on the
discard piles in the order they will be needed
to build on the foundations, i.e. in the
reverse of the order shown above. Also, it is
advisable to scatter cards of the same rank
throughout the different discard piles.
In practice, many of the cards turned up
from the stock will enable the player to
build on the foundation cards.

● If a discard pile runs out, the space can be
filled with a new pile, if required. The
maximum number of discard piles at any
one time is four.

Tips
Choose carefully on which pile to throw an

unplayable card. As a rule, it pays to keep
high cards in one discard pile or at the
bottom of more than one pile. Cards of low
to moderate rank are best spread among the
piles.

◆ CONTENDING KNIGHTS
A simple game of chance in which the four
Js win points against each other.

Cards

One standard deck of 52 cards.

The layout

The four Js are laid out in a row in the
following order: heart, club, diamond,
spade.

Aim

To play three rounds, allotting even-
numbered cards to the red Js and odd ones
to the black Js, and awarding points to each
J accordingly to determine a winner.

Playing

● Four cards are turned up from the stock
and placed on the table. If any are even-
numbered, regardless of suit or sequence,
they are placed in a pile near the J of hearts,
face up. Qs count as odd numbers, Ks as

even. More cards are turned up from the stock to replace any used.

● Any odd-numbered cards are piled near the J of clubs.

● The process is continued for the J of diamonds and the J of spades. Returning to the J of hearts again, play continues until all the stock has been used up.

● If a J cannot take any card in its turn, play

Playing on the layout for Contending Knights

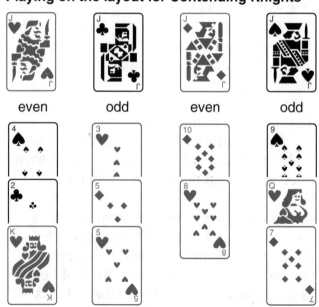

passes to the next J. If a J takes all four
cards, because they are all odd or all even,
that J is given one card from each of the
other three Js, regardless of whether they are
odd or even.

● When the stock is played out, a J whose
pile has 12 cards or more scores one point
for each card in excess of 12.

● The cards should be shuffled thoroughly
before playing the next round.

● When three rounds have been played, the
winner is the J with the highest number of
points.

◆ DOUBLE OR QUITS

A relatively easy mathematical game where
the chances of winning are slightly less than
the chances of losing. The game gets its
name from the nature of the sequence which
is built.

Cards

One standard deck of 52 cards.

The layout

Deal two columns of three cards each and
then deal a card between the columns at the
top. These seven cards are the reserve. One

card is then dealt between the columns at the
bottom. This is the one and only foundation.

A sample layout

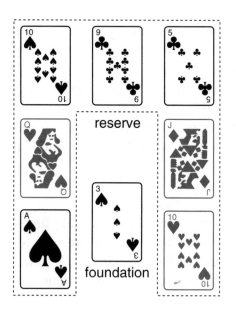

reserve

foundation

Aim

To build all the cards, other than the Ks, on
to the foundation card in a continuous
mathematical sequence.

Playing

● If any Ks turn up in the layout, remove
them and place them on the bottom of the
stock. Deal additional cards from the stock
to replace them.

● Turn up the cards from stock one by one,
and build upon the foundation, ignoring
suits, in the following sequence: ace, 2, 4, 8,
3, 6, Q, J, 9, 5, 10, 7, ace, 2 and so on (this
is a doubling sequence, where 13 is
subtracted each time the result exceeds 12).
So, if a 3 is the foundation card, the
sequence is built by adding 6, then Q, J and
so on.

● Play cards to the foundation sequence
from stock, or from the reserve. If the stock
card is unplayable, place it face up on a
discard pile, the top card of which is always
available for play.

● Any spaces in the reserve are filled from
the top of the discard pile or, if there is
none, from the stock. A K once placed in the
reserve (except at the start) must stay there.

● Two redeals (without shuffling) are
allowed.

◆ FLOWER GARDEN

The large layout for this game is called the
flower garden, individual fans of cards
being the 'flowerbeds' and reserve cards the
'bouquet'.

Cards

One standard deck of 52 cards.

The layout

Six fans of six cards each are dealt to form
the flowerbeds. The bouquet is the
remaining stock, which may be held in the
hand as a fan or spread face up on the table.
It can be sorted into suits.

Aim

To free the four aces and use them as
foundations to build upwards in suits, ace
to K.

Playing

● In the sample layout, the two aces in the
bouquet would immediately be placed face
up below the fans, starting two of the
foundations.

● Any card from the bouquet or any exposed
card from the ends of the flowerbeds can be
played. A card may be used to build
numerically upwards in suits on a

A sample layout

six flowerbeds

foundations

bouquet of 16 reserve cards

foundation ace, or to build downwards on
the exposed card of any flowerbed,
disregarding suit.

● As long as the numerical order remains
correct, a sequence of cards may be moved
from one flowerbed to another.

● When a bed is used up, its space may be
filled by one card from the bouquet or a bed,
or by a sequence from another bed.

Tip

Where possible, try to avoid using bouquet
cards for building in the flowerbeds.

◆ **FOURTEEN OUT**

A simple discard game. The game is also

A sample layout

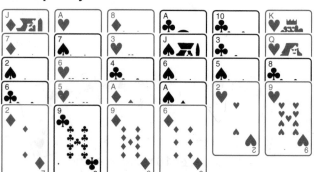

called Fourteen Puzzle or Take Fourteen. It requires a moderately large space.

Cards

One standard 52-card deck. If space is limited, use small cards.

The layout

Deal the cards, face up, in four rows of 12 cards each to form 12 columns of overlapping cards. The four remaining cards are added to the first four columns.

Aim

To discard the whole layout in pairs of cards that total 14.

Playing

● Only the top card of each column is available, but the other cards in each column

are visible to enable forward planning.

• Available cards are removed in pairs whose totals add up to 14: ace and K, 2 and Q, 3 and J, 4 and 10, 5 and 9, 6 and 8, 7 and 7.

◆ GRANDFATHER'S CLOCK

An easy game requiring a lot of space. This is the classic game with this title. Rather confusingly, some other similar games use the same title.

Cards

One standard 52-card deck. If space is limited, use small cards.

The layout

The following 12 cards are removed from the deck: 2H, 3S, 4D, 5C, 6H, 7S, 8D, 9C,

A sample layout

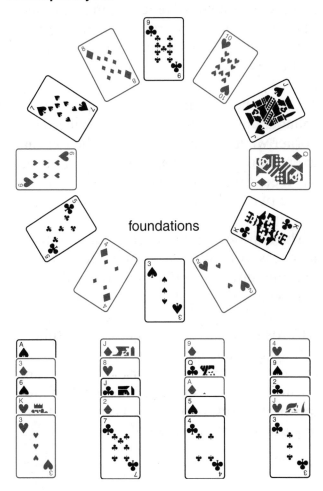

foundations

10H, JS, QD, KC. These cards are placed in a circle, as shown. The remaining cards are placed face up in five rows of eight cards each, with the cards overlapping to form eight columns.

Aim

To build the suits in rank order upon the 12 foundations of the clock face (turning the corner where necessary) so that the top card at each position corresponds to the time on the face: ace at the one o'clock position, two at the two o'clock, and so on.

Playing

● The exposed card of each column in the layout is available for play on a foundation building upwards within suit, or on the exposed card of another column, building downwards regardless of colour or suit.

● Cards may only be moved one at a time.

● A space made by playing off a whole column may be filled by any available card.

● Building on a foundation stops when the top card corresponds to the hour at that position on the clock face.

◆ KING ALBERT

King Albert I of Belgium lent his name to this game.

Cards

A standard deck of 52 cards.

The layout

Nine cards are dealt face up in a row to form nine columns. Cards are dealt onto the columns in rows, from left to right, so that there is one card in the first column, two cards in the second, three in the third and so on. There will be nine cards in the last column. (See sample layout overleaf.) Cards should overlap slightly and leave only the bottom card in each column fully exposed. The last seven cards form the reserve and are spread face up in a fan. Space is also required for four foundations (the aces).

Aim

To release the four aces during play and build upon them in suits in ascending order up to K.

Playing

● All cards in the reserve and the exposed bottom card in each column are available for play.

A sample layout

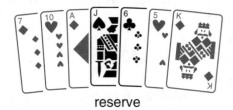

reserve

nine columns

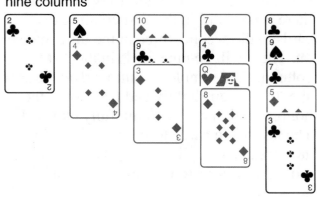

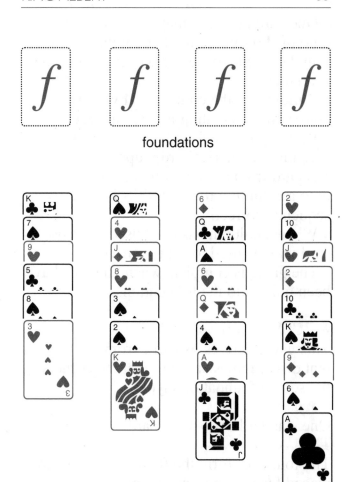

foundations

● One card at a time may be moved either
onto the bottom of another column or onto a
foundation pile once the aces have become
available.

● Building on the columns is by alternate
colours in descending numerical order.

● Building on the foundations is by suit in
ascending numerical order up to K.

● A card from a foundation may be moved
onto a column, provided it fits into the
sequence correctly.

● When a column has been used up, any
card may be used to fill the space.

● The game is complete when all cards have
been built onto the foundations.

◆ PUSS IN THE CORNER

This game derives its name from the fact
that discard piles are placed at the corners of
the square foundation layout.

Cards

One standard deck of 52 cards.

The layout

The four aces form the foundations and are
placed face up in a square arrangement.
Leave space around them for discard piles.

A sample layout

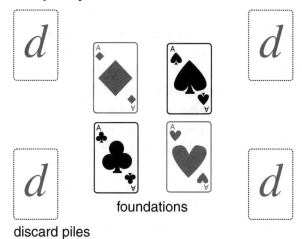

foundations

discard piles

Aim

To build numerically upwards on each
foundation, from ace to K, in the same colour
but disregarding suit.

Playing

● Cards are turned up from stock one at a
time and played onto a foundation, if
possible, or put face up onto any discard pile.
● It is best to keep one discard pile for the
high-ranking court cards and to avoid putting
high-ranking cards on top of those of low
rank.

● The top card on each discard pile is always available for play, but cards may not be moved from one discard pile to another.

● If the stock runs out before the game is resolved, one redeal is allowed.

● The four discard piles are gathered up in any order and used as the stock without shuffling. It is helpful to remember which cards are in which discard pile when collecting them.

◆ QUADRILLE

A simple game with an unusual layout, Quadrille is also known as Captive Queens.

Cards

One standard 52-card deck.

The layout

The layout is created as the game unfolds. The 5s and 6s form the foundation cards placed around the four Qs. The Qs play no role in the game and are there to add a touch of elegance to the layout.

Aim

To build the 6s up in suit to Js, and the 5s down in suit to Ks (5, 4, 3, 2, ace, K).

A sample layout

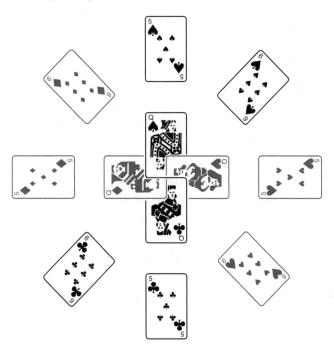

Playing
● The cards are turned up one at a time from the stock and if a 5 or 6 are placed as foundations; if Qs they are placed in the centre of the foundations as above.
● All other discards are placed face up on a single discard pile.

● Once a foundation card is in position it can be built upon within suit from stock. Foundation 6s are built up to Js; 5s are built down to Ks (turning the corner).

● The top card of the discard pile is always available.

● Two redeals of the discard pile are allowed, without shuffling.

◆ QUEEN'S AUDIENCE

When the king is the reigning monarch the game is called King's Audience. The game has an unusual layout and rules.

Cards

One standard 52-card deck.

The layout

Sixteen cards are dealt so as to enclose a square, with four cards to each side. These cards form a reserve called the Queen's Antechamber, and the space enclosed is the Queen's Audience. As the game unfolds, the Js go into the Audience and form the foundations.

Aim

To build upon the foundations within suit in descending rank order from J to 2.

A sample layout during play

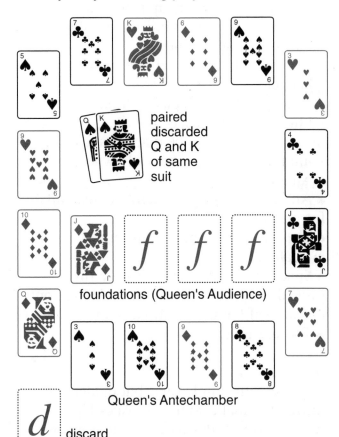

paired
discarded
Q and K
of same
suit

foundations (Queen's Audience)

Queen's Antechamber

discard
pile

Playing

- The cards are turned up from the stock one at a time; unplayable cards are put face up on a single discard pile.
- A J can only be placed as a foundation when an ace of the same suit is also available. The ace is placed under the J within the Audience. Similarly, Qs and Ks of the same suit can be placed as discards within the Audience, but only when both are available.
- All cards in the Antechamber are available for play on foundations.
- The top card of the discard pile is always available.
- Spaces in the Antechamber are filled immediately from the discard pile, or from the stock if there is no discard pile.
- There is no redeal.

◆ ACES UP

A game with simple rules but moderately difficult to make come out. Aces Up requires very little space. Its other names include Firing Squad or Idiot's Delight.

Cards

One standard 52-card deck.

The layout

Deal a single row of four cards face up. As the game progresses, add cards to form four columns of overlapping cards.

A sample layout

Aim

To discard all cards except the aces.

Playing

● Aces are high, ranking above Ks. Among the four available cards, if two cards are of the same suit, the one that is lower in rank is discarded. The space made available is filled with a card dealt from the hand.

● When all first round moves are complete, another row of four cards is dealt on top of the remaining four.

● Play continues as before, discarding all lower available cards when a higher card of the same suit is at the top of another pile.

● In the second and subsequent rounds of play, spaces are filled with an available card from one of the columns. Such moves make buried cards available.

● Exposed aces are not discarded but are moved into spaces. The rounds continue as before, dealing four cards each time, with the game being resolved when only four aces remain, the rest of the pack having been discarded.

● If all cards have been dealt, and the game blocks, the game is lost.

◆ BARONESS

Baroness is also called Five Piles or Thirteens. It requires little space.

Cards

One standard 52-card deck.

The layout

Deal a row of five cards face up.

A sample layout

Aim
To discard the whole pack in pairs that add
up to 13.

Playing
● Any available Ks (value 13) are discarded
plus any pair of cards, irrespective of suit,
that add up to 13: ace and Q, 2 and J, 3 and
10, 4 and 9, 5 and 8, 6 and 7.
● After moves are completed, the next row
of five cards is dealt on top of the first row,
and the discard process repeated with only
the top card of each pile available.
● When you get to the bottom of the stock,
the last two cards are turned face up and are
available.
● The game is won only if the whole pack
can be discarded in 13s.

◆ BETSY ROSS
A mathematical game of moderate difficulty
related to Calculation (p.18) but with less
scope for planning. The game requires a
moderate amount of space. Its other names
include Fairest, Four Kings and Musical.

Cards
One standard 52-card deck.

The layout

Any ace, 2, 3 and 4 are laid out as the top
row, and any 2, 4, 6 and 8 laid out directly
below as the bottom row. The four cards on
the bottom row are the foundations, but are
built upon in an unusual way. The four cards
in the top row are simply there as reminders
indicating how the cards of the bottom row
should be built upon.

A sample layout

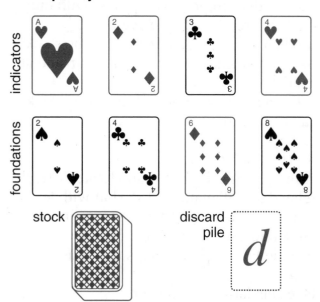

Aim

To build four different mathematical sequences of 12 cards on the foundations.

Playing

● Turn up cards from the stock one at a time, putting each either on a foundation, or face up on a single discard pile. The top of the discard pile is always available.

● Cards are built upon the foundations, irrespective of suit, as follows:

The 2 is built upon in the usual way at intervals of one as indicated by the ace. The entire sequence is 2, 3, 4, 5, 6, 7, 8, 9, 10, J, Q, K.

The 4 is built upon at intervals of two, to create the sequence 4, 6, 8, 10, Q, ace, 3, 5, 7, 9, J, K.

The 6 is built upon at intervals of three, to form the sequence 3, 6, 9, Q, 2, 5, 8, J, ace, 4, 7, 10, K.

The 8 is built upon at intervals of four to give the sequence 8, Q, 3, 7, J, 2, 6, 10, ace, 5, 9, K.

● Two redeals of the discard pile (without shuffling) are allowed.

◆ BISLEY

A game related to Baker's Dozen (p.14) but
more challenging. It requires a moderately
large amount of space.

Cards

One standard deck of 52 cards. Use small
cards if space is limited.

A sample layout

foundation aces

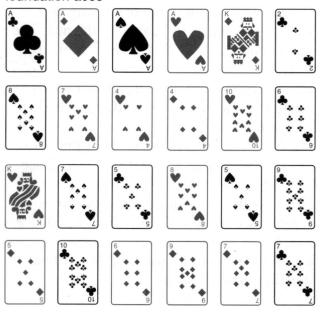

The layout
First place the four aces in a row on the
table, then increase the length of the row by
nine cards dealt from the pack. Continue to
deal the cards, making three more rows
below the first one, until you have four
rows, each of 13 cards.

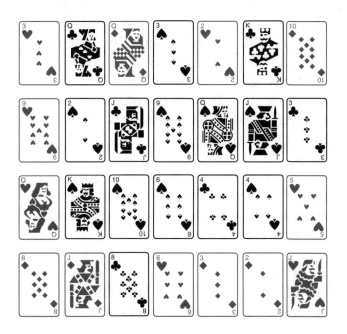

Aim

To build suits in rank order, using the aces
and the Ks as foundation cards.

Playing

● Any of the bottom row of cards can be used
to build on an ace of the same suit,
numerically upwards, or to build onto
another bottom-row card of the same suit,
either upwards or downwards.

● When a K becomes available, it is placed in
a new row above the ace of the same suit and
can then be built on numerically downwards.

● When the two sequences of one suit meet,
they can be put into one pile.

● Spaces at the bottom of columns are not
filled, thereby making the cards above them
available for play.

Tips

If you can, avoid building down on a column
in which a lower card of the same suit is
buried, or building up on a column in which
a higher card is buried.

◆ BRISTOL

Bristol combines the good qualities of
several other patience games.

Cards

One standard 52-card deck.

The layout

Eight fans of three cards each are dealt face up. Any Ks are placed at the bottom of the respective fans. Finally, three cards are dealt face up in a row to start three reserve piles. Aces, when they become available, are placed above the fans as foundations.
(See sample layout overleaf.)

Aim

To build four sequences in ascending numerical order from ace, the foundation card, up to K, disregarding the suits.

Playing

● Any top card from the reserve piles or the fans can be played, one at a time only.
The chosen card can be played in ascending numerical order onto a foundation or in descending numerical order onto the top card of a fan, disregarding suit.

● After moves are exhausted, three cards are dealt face up from the stock, one to each reserve pile. This refills any spaces left by an empty pile.

● When fans are used up, they are not replaced.
● There is no redeal.

A sample layout for Bristol

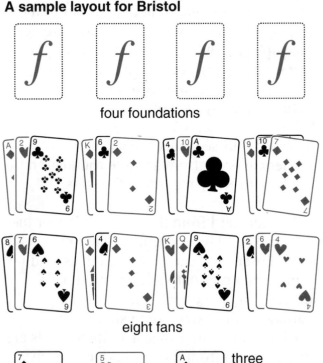

four foundations

eight fans

three
reserve
piles

◆ DUCHESS

Essentially, a one-deck version of the Queen of Italy (p.166). It is also called Glenwood.

Cards

One standard 52-card deck.

The layout

Deal four fans of three cards each at the top of the table as the reserve. Leave a space for four foundations, and then deal a row of four cards below.

A sample layout

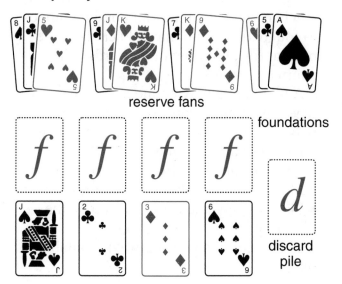

reserve fans

foundations

discard pile

Aim

To build the suits in rank order upon the four foundations (turning the corner where necessary).

Playing

● Choose the top card of one of the reserve fans to be the first foundation, and move the card into position.

● Put other cards of the same rank, as they become available, alongside the first foundation card in a row. Build upon these foundations within suit.

● When you have made all possible moves to foundations, you may add cards to the bottom row, building downwards using alternate colours.

● A whole pile may be moved as one unit when the bottom card of the pile is correct in colour and sequence for building on the top card of another pile.

● Turn up cards one by one from stock and build to the foundations or the piles.

● Place unplayable cards face up on the discard pile.

● The top of this pile is always available for play.

● The top cards of the reserve fans are available for building on foundations or layout piles, and are also available for filling spaces in the layout.

● When the fans are exhausted, fill spaces using the top card of the discard pile.

● One redeal (without shuffling) is allowed.

◆ EIGHT AWAY

This game, also known as Eight Off, features a large layout of eight columns in which there must never be more than eight cards.

Cards

A standard deck of 52 cards.

The layout

Eight cards are dealt face up in a row. Five more rows of eight cards are dealt face up, each row overlapping the one above so that all cards can be seen. The last four cards are turned face up in a row below the columns to form the reserve. (See overleaf.)

Aim

To move the aces above the layout to form four foundations and build on them numerically upwards to K in the same suit as each ace.

A sample layout

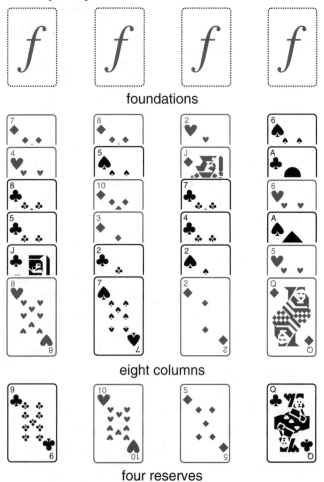

foundations

eight columns

four reserves

Playing

● The exposed card at the bottom of each column and the four reserve cards are available for play.

● Cards can be used to build upwards on the foundations or downwards in suits on any

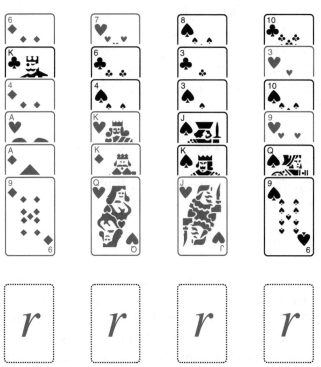

spaces for up to four more reserves

other exposed card, or they can be moved to
the reserve.

● Up to four more reserves can be made as
needed. The reserve and the columns must
each never contain more than eight cards.

● An empty column can only be replaced
with an available K.

Tips

Moving available cards from column to
reserve is a means of freeing a blockage.
Plan ahead and use reserve spaces in this
way.

◆ FLORENTINE

As in Vanishing Cross (p.92), the
moderately large layout of this game
incorporates a five-card cross.

Cards

A standard deck of 52 cards.

The layout

Five cards are turned face up and laid out to
form a cross. The sixth card is placed, face
up, at the top left corner of the table. This is
the first foundation card, and its rank
determines the rank of the other three
foundations, which will be placed at the

other three corners of the table as they come
up during play.

For example, if the first foundation is 7C,
then the other three foundations will be 7D,
7S, 7H. If one of these cards comes up
when forming the layout, or during play, it is
immediately placed in a foundation position.

A sample layout

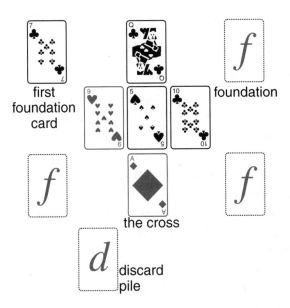

first
foundation
card

foundation

the cross

discard
pile

Aim

To build numerically upwards, in suits, on
the four foundation cards. The sequence from
a Q, K would be ace, 2, 3 and so on.

Playing

● One card at a time is played from the stock.
It can be used to build on the foundations. If
it is not suitable its suit is disregarded and it
can be placed, in downwards sequence, on
any of the four outer 'arms' of the cross. If
this is not possible, the card is placed face up
on a discard pile.

● Cards may not be played onto the central
card of the cross.

● When a card has been played from the
stock, suitable outer cards from the cross may
be used to build on the foundations, or on
each other.

● Spaces in the arms of the cross are filled by
the central card or a card from the discard
pile. When the central card is used, it is
replaced by the top card from the discard
pile.

● When the stock is exhausted, the discard
pile can be turned over, without shuffling,
and used once as the stock.

◆ LA BELLE LUCIE

A classic game. Cards are placed in fan shapes creating an attractive layout. The game's other names include The Fan and Alexander The Great.

Cards

A standard 52-card deck.

The layout

Deal all the cards face up into 17 fans of three cards each. The remaining card is dealt face up alone. (See sample layout overleaf.)

Aim

To release the four aces as foundations on which to build, in suits and in ascending numerical order, ace up to K.

Playing

● The single card and the exposed card of each fan are available to be played.

● One card at a time only is moved, either to build onto a foundation, once the aces have been released, or to build within suit downwards on the top card of a fan.

● Building down onto a fan should be done with care as any cards underneath will be inaccessible.

● Spaces left by the complete removal of

A sample layout for La Belle Lucie

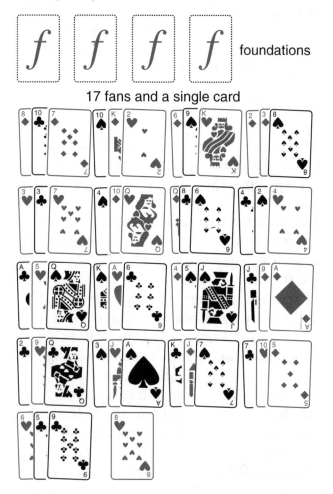

foundations

17 fans and a single card

fans are not filled. When the game becomes blocked because no more cards can be moved, all cards, except those already built onto foundations, are collected and shuffled. They are redealt into fans of three cards plus a pair or a single. Play then continues as before.

● If the game becomes blocked again, one more deal takes place, as before. After this second redeal there is a bonus. The first card to be played may be any card, even a buried one.

● No further redeal is then allowed.

◆ LEAPFROG

A game with unusual moves.

Cards

A standard 52-card deck is needed.

The layout

Deal four rows each with five separated face-up cards. The remaining stock is placed face down on the table. (See sample layout overleaf.)

Aim

To create as many unfilled spaces in the layout as possible, after using up the stock.

A sample layout for Leapfrog

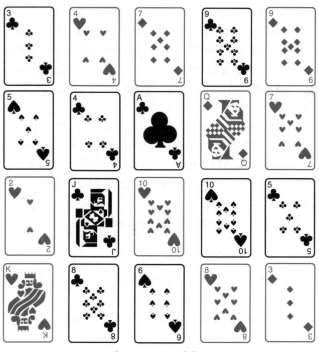

four rows of five

discard
pile

Playing

● Any card in the layout may 'leapfrog' over its neighbour in any direction horizontally, vertically or diagonally, as long as its destination is a card of the same rank or suit.

● The card that is leapt over is removed and placed face down on a discard pile.

● The two spaces created by a single leap are filled with face-up cards from the stock.

● A pile of two or more cards can also leapfrog according to the same rules; the top card of the pile is the identifying card.

● A card or a pile may also leapfrog several cards in succession, creating more spaces in one turn.

● When the stock is exhausted, the aim is to make as many spaces as possible before the game is blocked.

◆ LITTLE SPIDER

An interesting game with a compact layout. Played skilfully, it comes out more often than not. It gets its name from the eight piles – the eight legs of a spider.

Cards

One standard 52-card deck.

The layout

Deal four cards face up in a row, and then, leaving a space for a middle row, deal four cards face up to form a bottom row. As the game progresses, the foundation cards – two aces of one colour and two Ks of another colour – are placed in their appropriate places in the middle row.

Aim

To build up the foundation aces in suit to Ks and to build down the foundation Ks in suit to aces.

Playing

● Any card can be moved from the top row onto the foundations.

● A card from the bottom row cannot be moved up to the middle row unless it is directly below its appropriate place. For example, if from a previous move a red ace occupies the first foundation position, then the third and fourth positions must be filled by black Ks. A black K can be moved up from the bottom row only if it is position three or four and the space above it is free.

A sample layout

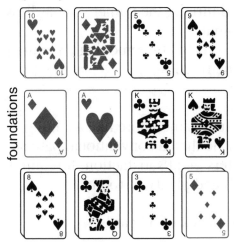

foundations

● After the first eight cards have been dealt, the player attempts to make moves – placing the foundations and then building upon them – using the above conventions.

● Another eight cards are dealt, and the process is repeated, and then again and again until all the cards are dealt.

● When the deal is complete, the special conventions no longer apply, and any exposed card from the top or bottom row can be built upon a pile in the middle row. Also, exposed cards in the top and bottom rows can be built upon one another – up or down, and turning the corner – regardless of suit or colour.

● A space created by removing an entire pile may not be filled.

◆ MAZE

This unusual game, more like a sliding block puzzle than a conventional patience game, offers great satisfaction. It requires time, skill and plenty of room.

Cards

A standard deck of 52 cards.

Layout

All the cards are dealt face up: two rows of eight cards above, and four rows of nine cards below. The four Ks are removed, leaving six empty spaces in the layout. (See sample layout overleaf.)

Aim

To rearrange the cards, one at a time, so that all cards are in suit sequences, ace to Q, from left to right. The suits can be in any order – for example, ace S to QS, followed by diamonds, hearts and clubs, each in sequence.

The cards may occupy any of the positions in the six rows, but rows may not be extended beyond their original length. A sequence may begin anywhere, each line following on from the end of the one above. The bottom line runs on to the beginning of the top line.

Playing

● Any card can be moved into any of the spaces created by the discarded Ks, provided it makes a correct in suit sequence with one of its new neighbours. For example, 6D can only be moved to a space with 5D on its left or 7D on its right.

● A space at the beginning or end of a row is regarded as flanked by the card next to it and by the card at the end of the row above or the one at the beginning of the row below. If a space occurs to the right of a Q, it may be filled with any ace, even if there is not yet a neighbouring 2.

● Where two spaces are next to one another, only one card is capable of filling either.

● Where three or more spaces are next to one another, the spaces in the middle cannot be occupied. Success can be achieved by thinking ahead before making a move.

A sample layout with Ks removed

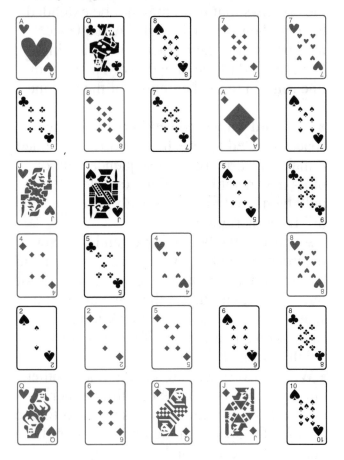

◆ MONTE CARLO

A discard game requiring a moderate
amount of space. Monte Carlo is also known
as Weddings, referring to the discarding of
cards in pairs.

Cards

One standard 52-card deck.

The layout

Five rows of five cards each are dealt to
form a square layout.

Aim

To discard the entire pack in pairs of the
same rank.

Playing

● Within the layout, cards of the same rank
are discarded if they are lying next to each
other; either side-by-side, directly above or
below, or diagonally adjacent.

● After removing all possible pairs, spaces
in the layout are filled by moving the cards
forward in the layout in the same order in
which they were dealt.

● New cards are then dealt to fill the bottom
rows of the layout and the discard process is
repeated.

● The procedure – discard, close up and deal

– is continued until all cards from stock have been dealt.

A sample layout after initial deal

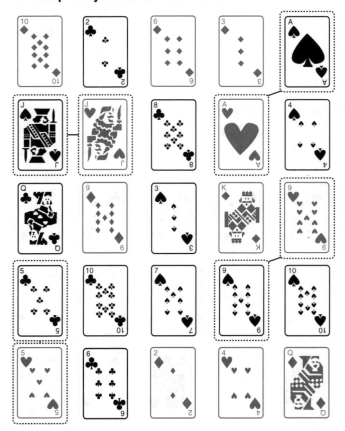

● To win, the entire pack must be discarded in adjacent matched pairs – a challenging task.

Layout for Monte Carlo after first filling deal

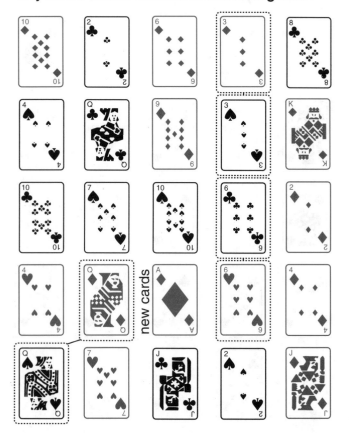

◆ NESTOR

Nestor, like Monte Carlo (p.72), is a game where cards are discarded in pairs of the same rank. Sometimes called Matrimony, it requires a moderate amount of space.

Cards

One standard 52-card deck. If space is limited, use small cards.

The layout

Eight cards are dealt face up in a row. Then another five rows are dealt in a similar manner but overlapping the cards to form eight columns. When dealing, ensure that there are no two cards of the same rank in the same column. For example, if a three is about to be dealt onto a column which already contains a three, then the three in the hand is put to the bottom of the stock and the next card is dealt to the column instead. When the rows and columns are complete, the four cards left over are the stock. (See sample layout overleaf.)

Aim

To discard the whole pack in pairs.

Playing

● Cards of the same rank are discarded in

pairs from the exposed cards at the end of
the columns.

● If moves are exhausted, turn up the first
card of the stock to see if it will match any
of the exposed cards on the layout and so
unblock one of the columns.

A sample layout

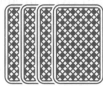

● The game is lost if the topmost stock card
cannot be used when needed.
Note: An alternative form of the game has
all four stock cards face up as a reserve.
They are available at any time.

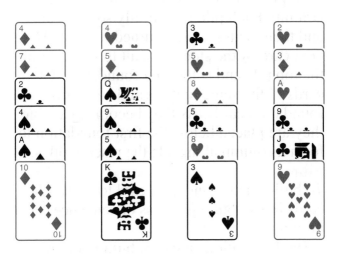

◆ OSMOSIS

A popular building game requiring a moderate amount of space and plenty of time. It is also called Treasure Trove.

Cards

One standard 52-card deck.

The layout

Four piles of four cards each are dealt in a column. Each pile is carefully squared up and then the top card is turned face up. The next card of the stock is dealt to the right of the top pile and is the first foundation. Other cards of the same rank form the other three foundation cards. As they become available they are placed below the first foundation to form a column alongside the reserve piles.

Aim

To build each foundation card to a full 13 cards in suit but regardless of sequence.

Playing

● The foundation cards are built upon in suit, regardless of order, but no card may be placed in the second, third or fourth foundation rows unless a card of the same rank has already been placed on the foundation card in the previous row.

A sample layout after several plays

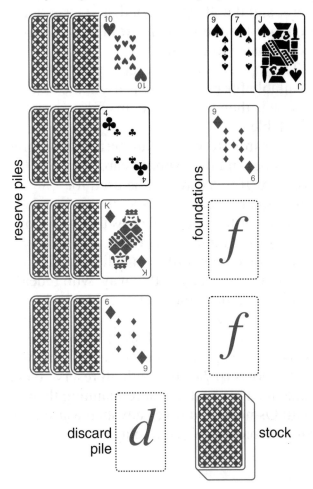

reserve piles

foundations

discard pile

stock

For example, if the 9S is the first foundation card, and the 9D the second, a 7D can only be placed in the second row after a 7S has been placed in the first.

● The top cards of the reserve piles are available for play. If one is used, the card below is then turned face up and becomes available.

● The cards from stock are turned over three at a time, and the exposed card is available for play. If this card can be used for building, it releases the second card, and the second card, if used, releases the third. Any or all of the three cards, if not used, are placed face up in order on a discard pile.

● Play is continued in this way, with redeals, until the game comes out or is blocked.

◆ **PEEK (A VARIANT OF OSMOSIS)**
This game is played in exactly the same way as Osmosis (p.78), but with all reserve cards face up. This enables more planning than with Osmosis and gives advance warning of an unavoidable block to play.

A sample layout after several plays

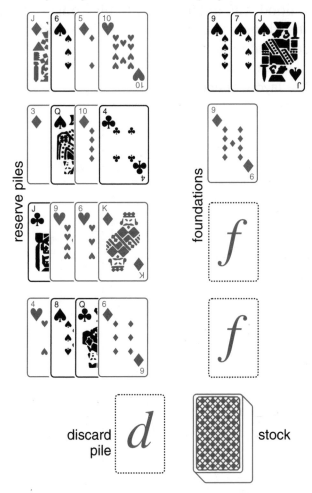

◆ POKER SOLITAIRE

A good way to learn how to play poker, this
absorbing game requires good luck and
good judgement.

The layout spaces

Cards
One standard 52-card deck.

The layout
Space will be needed for five rows of five cards, which will be dealt face up during play. Each row and each column is called a poker hand. There will be space for ten hands.

Aim
To place cards anywhere in the rows and the columns to give the highest possible poker score, using either the British or the American scoring system.

Playing
● As the cards are turned up from the stock they may be placed anywhere on the layout.
● Ace can rank high or low but may not be used to turn the corner, i.e. K, ace, 2 is not permitted.

Other rules
1 The joker may be included in the deck and can represent any card. It may simply be added to the stock before dealing or may be used to replace a card after the deal has been played.
2 The 25 cards can be dealt out in the order

they are turned up and then can be
rearranged to make the best hands.

3 A more difficult variation is to limit the
placing of each card to a position
neighbouring the last one: side, top, bottom
or diagonal.

The nine hands	
Name	**Combination**
Royal flush	10, J, Q, K, ace of the same suit
Straight flush	5-card sequence in same suit
Four of a kind	4 cards of one rank + 1 odd card
Full house	3 same-rank cards + 2 of another rank
Flush	5 cards of one suit
Straight	any 5-card sequence
Three of a kind	3 same-rank cards + 2 odd cards
Two pairs	2 pairs + 1 odd card
One pair	1 pair + 3 odd cards

The scoring systems

Name of hand	American score	British score
Royal flush	100	30
Straight flush	75	30
Four of a kind	50	16
Full house	25	10
Flush	20	5
Straight	15	12
Three of a kind	10	6
Two pairs	5	3
One pair	2	1
None of the above	0	0

● An excellent score would be
  200 (American) or 60 (British).

◆ SCORPION
This game does have a sting in its tail,
because if the hidden cards are not revealed
early, they can block further moves towards
the end of the game.
Cards
One standard 52-card deck.
The layout
Deal a row of seven cards, the first four face

A sample layout

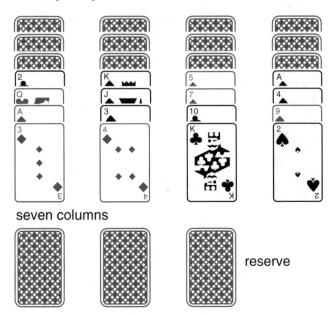

seven columns

reserve

down and the last three face up. Deal two
more rows in the same way, each
overlapping the previous row. Finally, deal
four more rows of cards all face up.
The three remaining cards are the reserve
and are placed face down below the rows.
The four Ks will be the foundation cards.
They are not removed from the layout.

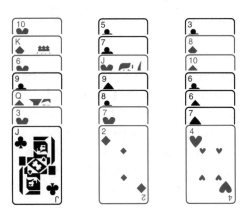

Aim

To build on the Ks in suits in descending order, down to the aces.

Example of play

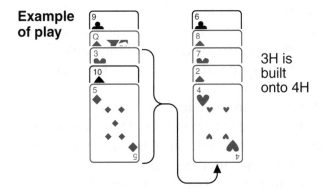

3H is built onto 4H

Playing

● Building can only take place on fully
exposed cards, i.e. the bottom card in each
column.

● Any appropriate card in the layout can be
used to build and takes with it cards below it
in the column. For example, if 4H is
exposed, 3H can be built onto it together
with all its overlapping cards, as shown on
the previous page. This move also leaves
a Q available for building.

● Aces cannot be built on.

If a face-down card is exposed, it can then
be turned over and is available for play. It is
best to try and release the face-down cards
early in the game to improve the chances of
completing all the building.

● When a column has been cleared, the space
may be filled by a K, plus all the cards
below it. Spaces do not have to be filled
immediately.

● Reserve cards are turned up only when no
further moves are possible. They can only
be added to the bottom of the three left-hand
columns. Provided no other moves are
possible, the reserve can be turned up before

any column spaces are filled, giving the player greater choice.

◆ THREE BLIND MICE

A game with straightforward rules that comes out about one time in ten by an enjoyable combination of luck and skill. It often blocks at an advanced stage in the game, to your aggravation or bemusement.

Cards

One standard 52-card deck.

The layout

Deal a row of ten cards with the first seven cards face up and the last three face down. Repeat this procedure with a second row of cards, and then a third, both overlapping the first row. Then add two more overlapping rows in which all the cards are face up. The result is ten columns each containing five overlapping cards. The last three columns each contain three cards face down and two face up. Place the two cards left over face up to one side as a reserve. (See overleaf.)

Aim

To build all four suits in descending order from K to ace within the layout.

A sample layout and moves

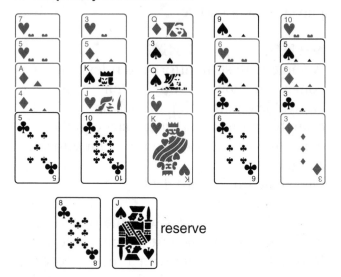

reserve

Playing

● Only exposed cards can be built upon.
However, cards used for building can come
from anywhere in any other column, but
may not come from within the column of the
build.

● If there are other cards on top of the one
being used for building, they are carried
with the moved card. For example, in the
layout shown, the QH can be built on the

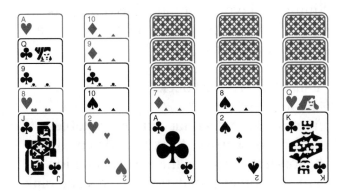

KH, taking the KC with it and releasing a
buried face-down card.

● Face-down cards become available only
when uncovered. The two reserve cards can
be played whenever you wish.

● When one of the face-down cards is
uncovered, it is turned over and becomes
available for play.

● A space created by removing an entire
column is filled with a K and any other
cards the K carries with it.

Tips

Aim to uncover the buried face-down cards
as soon as you reasonably can.

◆ VANISHING CROSS

Similar in layout to Florentine (p.58), its
other names include Corner Card, Czarina
and Four Seasons.

Cards

A standard 52-card deck.

The layout

Five cards are dealt face up on the table in
the form of a cross. A sixth card is dealt to
the top-left corner as the first foundation
card. The other foundations – the same rank
as the first foundation card – are placed in
the other corners as they become available
during play.

Aim

To build up the corner cards into the four
suits in rank order (turning the corner where
necessary).

Playing

● As cards of foundation rank become
available they are placed in the corners.

● From the layout, available cards are built
upwards in suit upon the foundations.

● Cards within the cross are built
downwards in rank order, regardless of

A sample layout

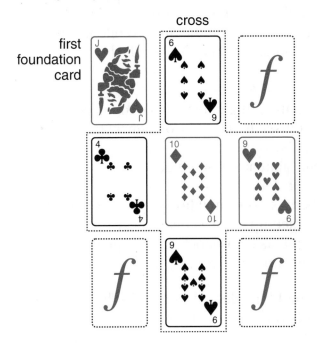

cross

first
foundation
card

colour and suit, and turning the corner
where necessary.

● When all possibilities are exhausted, the
top card of the stock is turned over and can
be played to the foundations, or to the cross.
It can be used to fill any spaces within the

cross. If unusable, the card is placed face up
on a discard pile.

● The top card of the discard pile is always
available, but there is no redeal.

✖ ACCORDION

A challenging game, also known as
Methuselah or Tower of Babel.

Cards

One standard 52-card deck.

The layout

There is no formal layout. A single row of
six face-up cards is dealt out. Surplus cards
are put aside as stock and are dealt as space
opens up.

Aim

To build the deck into one pile by matching
cards according to rank or suit.

Playing

● Any card can be moved onto the card on
its left or onto the third card from its left, if
it matches in rank or suit. For example, in
the sample layout the KS matches the KC
(on its left) and also the 2S (third to the
left). The KS can be moved to either position.

A sample layout

● Once moved, the new pile acts as a single card. The buried card is no longer in play but the top card is available to be matched.

● Other cards in the row can be added to this pile as long as they match the top card; and piles of cards can be moved in similar fashion, according to the rank and suit of the top card.

● When space becomes available, other cards can be added to the row in those spaces available.

● The game is resolved when a single pile has been made of all the cards. If further moves are impossible before this happens, all cards should be collected and shuffled for a new game.

✖ CANFIELD

Named in the USA after a 19th-century gambler and art collector, this game is often known in the UK as Demon. It requires a moderately large playing space.

Cards

One standard deck of 52 cards.

The layout

First a pile of 13 cards (the reserve) is dealt face down, then turned over leaving one card exposed.The next four cards are placed face up in a row next to the reserve; these form the base cards. The next card is placed above the first base card and forms the first of a row of four foundations. Its rank determines the rank of all the foundation cards. If a base card already dealt matches the foundation card, it is moved up into the foundation row, and another is dealt in its place. The remaining cards form the stock.

Aim

To build upwards, in suits, on the foundation cards, and to build downwards on the base cards, disregarding suit but in alternate colours, until all the cards are used from the

A sample layout

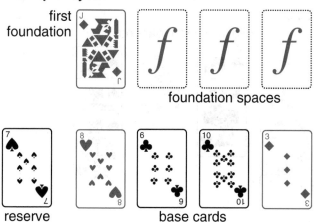

first foundation

foundation spaces

reserve   base cards

stock, the reserve and the discard pile (if there is one).

Playing

● Three cards at a time are dealt face up from stock. The top card is available for play and, once used or discarded, frees the next for play. The card may be played onto a foundation pile, a base pile or face up on the discard pile. If the card is the same rank as the first foundation card, it forms the next foundation.

● Building on the foundations is done

How the cards might be played

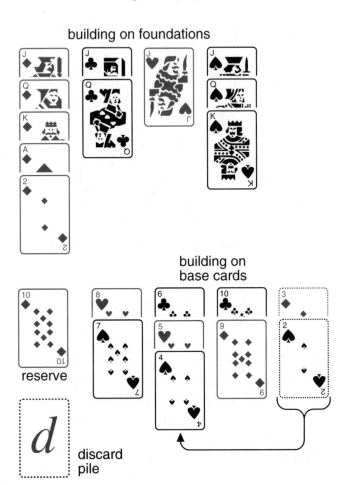

building on foundations

building on base cards

reserve

discard pile

numerically upwards, in suits, K followed by ace, 2, etc.

● Building on the base cards is done numerically downwards, in alternate colours of either suit. A sequence on a base card can be transferred to another base sequence, providing the colours still alternate and the sequence continues.

● The top card of the discard pile is always available for play on foundations or base piles.

● Cards from the reserve are used to fill spaces in the base. When the reserve is exhausted, the top card from the discard pile may be used to make a new base if required, or the base may be left empty.

● When fewer than three cards remain in the stock, they are dealt one at a time.

The discard pile may be redealt without shuffling. Redeals are repeated, until the game either comes out or becomes blocked.

✖ CLOCK

This game has many names, such as Sundial, Travellers, Four of a Kind and Hidden Cards. It is a fast-moving, enjoyable game, but the

chances of getting all the cards out are small.
Cards
A standard deck of 52 cards.
The layout
The cards are dealt face down, in 13 piles of
4 cards; 12 piles making a clock face and the
13th pile in the centre. The cards may be
dealt singly, dealing round the circle four
times, or in groups of four at a time.
Aim
To reorganise the cards so each pile is of the
same rank and matches the position of the
hours of the clock: aces at 1 o'clock, 2s at
2 o'clock and so on to Qs at 12 o'clock,
leaving the Ks in the central pile.
Playing
● The top card of the central pile is turned up
and placed under its appropriate position. For
example, an 8 would be placed under the 8
o'clock pile. The top card from that pile is
then turned up and correctly placed, and so on.
● If a card is turned up that belongs to the
same pile, the procedure is the same.
● If a K is turned up it is placed under the
central pile and the top card turned up and
used for play.

The layout for Clock

● When, during the game, the fourth face-up
card is added to a pile and there is no face-
down top card to pick up, the top card of the
next value pile is turned up. For example, if
the 8 o'clock pile is complete, the top card
of the 7 o'clock pile is turned face up, or if
that too is complete, the top card of the
6 o'clock pile is used, and so on.

• The game can only be resolved if the last card to be turned up is the fourth K. If the fourth K is turned up before all the other piles are complete, the game is lost. Consequently, players often repeat the game many times at great speed, hoping to win at least once!

✖ EAGLE WING

Eagle Wing is superficially similar to Canfield (p.96) but offers less scope for planning. The rules are straightforward, but the game is difficult to win. It is sometimes called Thirteen Down or Wings.

Cards

One standard 52-card deck.

The layout

Thirteen cards are dealt face down in a pile in the middle of the table. They form the reserve, known as 'the trunk'. Four cards are then dealt face up in a row to the left of the pile, and four cards face up to the right. These rows form the 'wings' of the eagle. One card is dealt face up directly above the trunk pile and is the first foundation card. The other foundations – the same rank as the original foundation – are placed in a row alongside the first as they become available. (See sample layout overleaf.)

Aim

To build the suits in rank order upon the four foundations (turning the corner where necessary).

Playing

● Cards in the wings are available for play to foundation spaces and for building upwards on foundations within suit, turning the corner where necessary.

● Any spaces created in the wings are then filled by turning over the topmost card of the trunk.

● When moves from the wings are exhausted, play continues using the topmost card of the stock. This may be played directly to a foundation and used for building upwards in suit. If unusable, the card is placed face up on a discard pile. The top of this pile is always available for play.

● The last card of the trunk may be played directly to the foundations without waiting for a place in the wings. When the trunk is exhausted, spaces in the wings are filled

A sample layout for Eagle Wing

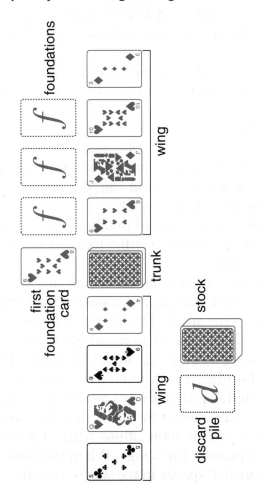

from stock or using the top card of the
discard pile.

● Two redeals (without shuffling) are
allowed.

✖ FORTRESS

Fortress, sometimes simply called Fort, is
related to Beleaguered Castle (p.16). It is
simple to play but difficult to win. It
requires a moderately large amount of space.

Cards

One standard 52-card deck.

The layout

A row of six overlapping cards is dealt face
up on either side of a playing space. Below
each row are dealt face up four rows of
overlapping cards, each containing five
cards. Foundation aces are placed in a
column in the centre of the layout as they
become available. (See layout overleaf.)

Aim

To build up the aces in suit to Ks.

Playing

● The exposed card at the end of each row is
available for play. Exposed cards are played
to the foundations, where possible,

beginning with aces. Cards can be built
within suit, one at a time, on exposed cards
in the layout. In such cases building is up or
down but not both ways in the same row.

A sample layout for Fortress

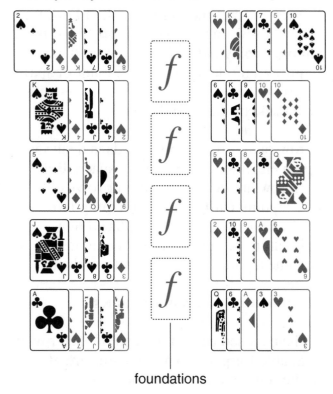

foundations

✘ FRIDAY THE THIRTEENTH

A game built on 13 foundations, requiring careful choices during play.

Cards

A standard deck of 52 cards.

The layout

Select any J, Q, K and ace and place them in a row in that order, left to right. These are the first four foundations. Space will be needed for another nine foundations, from 2 to 10. The remaining stock is kept face down. (See sample layout overleaf.)

Aim

To bring out nine more foundations while building piles of four cards upwards, in numerical order, on all 13 foundations, disregarding suit and colour.

Playing

● Turn up one card at a time from the stock. It may be used to build on an existing foundation or to become a new foundation.

● Foundations must be laid in correct rank order. A 2 must be laid down first, after which a 3 can be laid, and so on. If the option occurs, it is usually more helpful to

A sample layout for Friday the Thirteenth

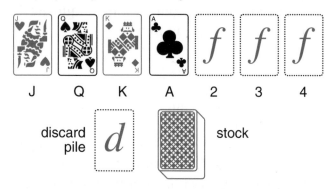

| J | Q | K | A | 2 | 3 | 4 |

discard pile d stock

put out a foundation card rather than to use it for building.

● Building on foundations must be done numerically upwards, until there are four cards in each pile. For example, on the Q build any K, ace, 2; on the 8 build any 9, 10, J.

● Cards may not be taken from one pile and used to build on another. If a card cannot be used, it is placed face up on the discard pile. The exposed card on the discard pile is always available for play.

● If the stock runs out, the discard pile is turned face down and used as the stock. This is allowed only once.

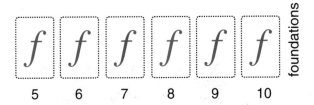

5   6   7   8   9   10

�֍ GAPS

Gaps, sometimes called Spaces, is related to Maze (p.68) but is harder to make come out. It requires a lot of space.

Cards

One standard 52-card deck. If space is limited, use small cards.

The layout

The entire pack is dealt face up in four rows of 13 cards each. The four aces are then removed to make gaps in the layout. (See sample layout overleaf.)

Aim

To build an entire suit (less the ace) in rank order within each row.

Playing

● The gaps in the layout are filled by the card that is next higher in rank to the card on

A sample layout

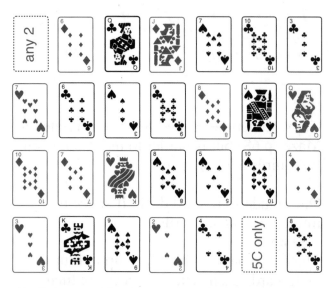

the left – and in the same suit. For example, if a gap opens up to the right of a 4C it must be filled by a 5C.

● If the gap opens up in the first space at the left of a row, it may be filled with any 2.

● If the gap opens up after a K, it cannot be filled and the row is blocked at that point.

● When a K blocks the moves in every row,

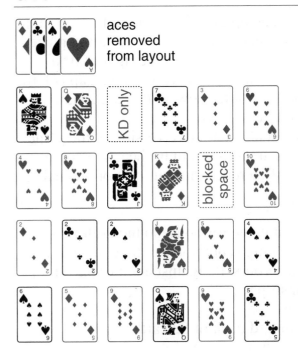

then that deal is over.

● Two shuffled redeals are allowed. Redeals are performed as follows. Leave in place any 2s that appear at the left end of a row and any cards that directly follow it and are in the correct order and suit. All other cards are removed from the layout, shuffled, and then dealt out again to fill up the rows but leaving a gap directly to the right of each in-suit sequence. If the only card left in place was a 2, a gap is left to the right of it. If there was no 2 in the row, then a gap is left at the start of the row so that a 2 can be moved in.

Note: In an alternative version of the game, redeals are allowed until the game comes out – often requiring four or more redeals.

✖ GOLF

A great game for housebound golfers.

By keeping score you can play the game against yourself, against another player, or against 'par'.

Cards

A standard deck of 52 cards.

The layout

Turn seven cards face up, placing them in a row to become the start of seven columns. Build the columns by placing another card face up below each one. Repeat until there are five cards in each of the seven columns, all clearly visible. This arrangement is called the links. The remaining 17 cards are placed face down in a pile and form the

A sample layout

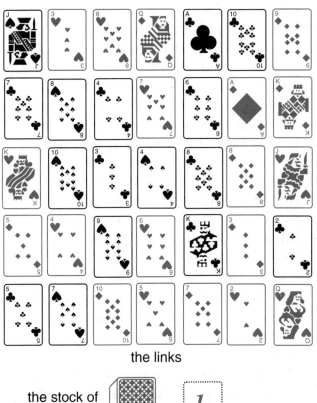

the links

the stock of
golf clubs the hole

stock of golf clubs.

Aim

To get the lowest possible score by using the stock of golf clubs to 'clear' the links. For a nine-hole round, the game would be played nine times.

Playing

● Turn one card face up from the stock to form the hole. Any card from the links may be played onto this card, regardless of colour or suit, providing it follows in numerical sequence, upwards or downwards. Ace counts as low, so the top card of a sequence would be a K.

● The direction can be reversed – for example, cards from the links might be available to build on a 3 in a downwards sequence, 2, ace, followed by an upwards sequence, 2, 3, 4, 5. There is no turning the corner.

● When it becomes impossible to play any more cards from the links, another card is turned up from the stock, placed on the hole and the process of building in sequence begins again.

● When there is a choice about which way to

build the sequence, it is helpful to remember which cards have already been played.

● When the stock is exhausted, the number value of the cards remaining on the links is totalled. J, Q, K count as 10 each. The total is the score for the hole. If the links have been cleared and no cards remain in the stock, the score is 0. As in golf, the lower the score the better.

● For a nine-hole game, the cards are shuffled and a new layout is dealt eight more times.

✖ KLONDIKE

An attractive, fast-moving game combining judgement and luck. This classic game is sometimes known in the UK as Canfield, not to be confused with the American game of that name described earlier.

Cards

A standard deck of 52 cards.

The layout

Deal one card face up and six more face down in a row from left to right. Along the next row, deal one card face up on the second column and five more face down on the remaining columns, partly overlapping the first row.

Along the next row deal one card face up on the third column and four more face down on the remaining four columns. Continue in this way until the last column has six face-down cards and one face-up card at the bottom.The undealt cards are held face down in the hand and form the stock.

Aim

To place the four aces as foundations when they become available during play and to build upon them in suits in ascending order up to K.

Playing

● Only one card is played at a time. It can be the top card from the stock or any of the exposed cards from the columns.

● Any card from the stock which cannot immediately be played is placed face up on a discard pile. The top card of this pile is available for play.

● A card may be placed onto an exposed card in the columns, in alternate colours and descending numerical order. Once the foundation aces are released during play,

A sample layout

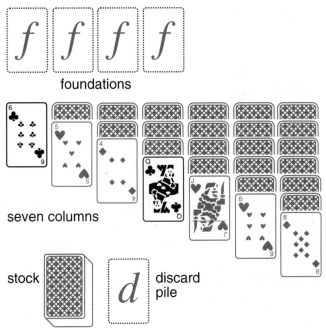

foundations

seven columns

stock   discard pile

cards may then be built onto them in suits in ascending numerical order.

● As a card is removed from a column, the next card is turned face up.

● When a column is used up, its space may only be occupied by a K. The K may be from anywhere in the layout and brings with it any cards already built onto it.

● Sequences may be transferred from one column to another as a complete unit.

● There is no redeal.

✖ PYRAMID

This game seems easy, but luck plays a big part.

Cards

One standard 52-card deck.

The layout

A pyramid shape is made by placing cards face up in seven rows, each row one card wider than the one before. Cards overlap, leaving only the bottom row of seven cards completely exposed and available at the start of play. Two discard piles are used.

Aim

To remove the entire pack from the game as pairs totalling 13.

Playing

● Ignoring colour and suit, cards make pairs if their values total 13. Ace is 1, Q 12 and J 11, so an ace and a Q make a pair; so do a J and a 2. Ks are worth 13 and are played alone.

● Play begins by turning up a card from the stock and either pairing it up with an

A sample layout

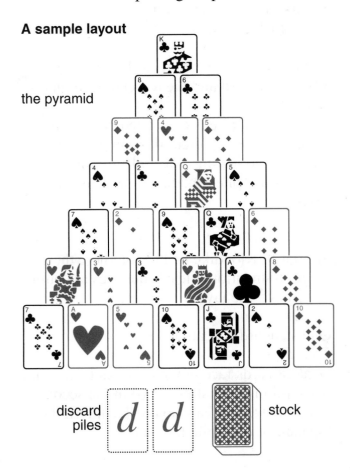

the pyramid

discard piles   *d*   *d*   stock

available card from the base of the pyramid
or placing it on either discard pile.

● Pairs may be made from:

1 the stock card and an available pyramid
card;

2 two available pyramid cards; or

3 the stock card and the top card of either
discard pile.

● If the stock pile is exhausted before all
cards have been paired, there may be one
redeal by collecting and shuffling together
both discard piles and using them as the
stock pile.

✖ SPIDERETTE

Similar to Klondike (p.115) but here there
are no foundation piles; sequences are built
directly on the layout.

Cards

One standard 52-card deck.

The layout

Deal 28 cards face down in seven piles, with
one card in the first pile, two in the second,
three in the third, and so on. Then turn the
top card of each pile face up.

A sample layout

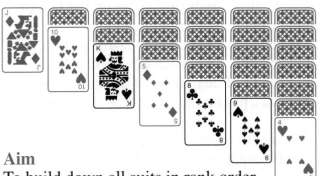

Aim

To build down all suits in rank order,
from K to ace, and then discard them.

Playing

● Exposed cards are built down in sequence,
regardless of suit or colour, but building
within suit wherever possible.

● Available cards are moved one at a time,
but within-suit sequences of cards can be
moved from one column to another when
building.

● When a face-down card is bared, it is
turned over and becomes available.

● When a space is created in the layout, this
is filled with any available card or within-
suit sequence.

● Whenever moves are exhausted, another seven cards are dealt face up on the layout, one on each column.

● When all 13 cards of one suit are in order in a column, the sequence is discarded.

● In the final deal, the last three cards from stock are put on the first three columns.

▼ AULD LANG SYNE

A classic patience game. Quick to play, it is maddeningly difficult to make come out.

Cards

One standard 52-card deck.

The layout

The four aces are placed face up in a row. They are the foundations. Underneath each ace is dealt a card. These cards are the reserve.

Aim

To build the suits in rank order upon the four foundation aces.

Playing

● Where possible, the exposed card of a reserve pile is built on an appropriate foundation.

● When moves, if any, are complete, four

more cards are dealt face up on the reserve
piles. Cards in the reserve piles become.
available when they are uncovered, but may
not be used to fill spaces.

● If the final cards from stock, and those
from the reserve, cannot be played to the
built sequences, the game is lost.

● There is no redeal.

A sample layout for Auld Lang Syne

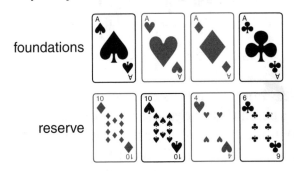

foundations

reserve

▼ HIT OR MISS

An unusual game without a layout. The
chances of success are small. Its other
names include Harvest, Roll Call and
Talkative.

Cards

One standard 52-card deck.

The layout
Cards are simply dealt face up to a pile.
Aim
To correctly call the name of a card, and then
discard it, until every card in the pack is
discarded.

A sample layout for Hit or Miss

stock   face up
pile

Playing
● The cards are dealt face up one at a time on
to a pile. As each card is turned over it is
named, starting with ace, two, three and so
on, through the ranks. The thirteenth card is
called a K and the fourteenth an ace.
● If the turned-up card corresponds with the
rank called, this is called a *hit*, and the card is
discarded rather than placed on the pile.
● Counting and discarding continue until the
stock is exhausted. Then the pile is picked up
and counting and discarding continue from

where you left off. The game continues in this way until all the cards are discarded (which is rare) or until the pack has been gone through twice in succession without a hit, at which stage the game is lost.

▼ PENDULUM

An unusual and fiendishly difficult patience game. Its title comes from the alternating moves – first to right, then to left. It requires plenty of space.

Cards

One standard 52-card deck. If space is limited, use small cards.

The layout

Remove the four aces and deal the remaining 48 cards face up in six non-overlapping rows of eight cards each. The layout is effectively eight columns of six cards. To the right of the layout place the four aces in a vertical column. These are the foundations. (See sample layout overleaf.)

Aim

To build the foundation aces up in suit to form four 13-card sequences. There is a choice of interval for building. It may be

A sample layout

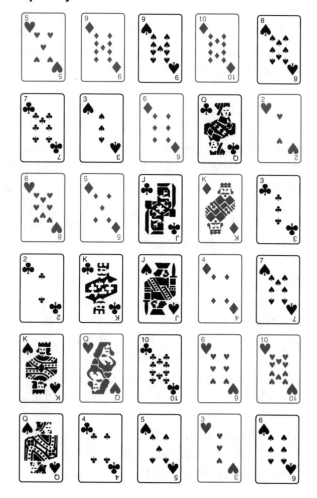

foundations

consecutive, i.e. ace, 2, 3 and so on, or some
other interval. For example, the sequences
may be built at intervals of three, giving the
order: ace, 4, 7, 10, K, 3, 6, 9, Q, 2, 5, 8, J.
Once the choice of interval is made, it is
fixed and cannot be changed. The chosen
interval applies to all four foundation
sequences.

Playing

● The bottom card of each column is
available for play to foundations.

● In addition, it may be built upon the card
immediately above it in its column, if that
card is of the same suit and next higher in
rank by the required interval. For example,
if the chosen interval is three, the 3H may be
built on the 6H as shown in the sample
layout.

● Two or more cards built in sequence in
this way may be added to the card directly
above if it properly continues the sequence.

● Also, any card or built sequence at the
bottom of a column may be built on the card
at either end of the top row, provided that it
properly continues the sequence.

● When a space is created by clearing out an

entire column, the space must be filled with
a card of the rank required to complete a 13-
card sequence: if the chosen interval is
three, this card would be a J. The move must
be made as soon as the card becomes
available.

Swinging the pendulum

Whenever play comes to a standstill, get it
moving again by 'swinging the pendulum'.
The first swing must be to the right, and
thereafter alternately to the left and right.
The swing is accomplished by moving the
cards in all rows that contain gaps (except
the top row) toward one side of the layout.
For example, when the swing is to the right,
the cards in a row are moved to the right,
thus shifting any spaces to the left-hand end
of the row. Swinging the pendulum in this
way creates new combinations of cards
within the columns.

Note: The top row is not 'swung' because its
first and last cards are special cards
available for building.

The pendulum may be swung as many times
as you wish until the game is won or it
becomes blocked (as is usually the case).

2. Games using a stripped single deck

● EVEN UP

A simple game of chance which comes out about one time in three.

Cards

A standard 52-card deck from which all the face cards – Js, Qs, Ks – have been removed.

The layout

The entire pack of 40 cards is dealt face up in a single row of overlapping cards.

A sample layout

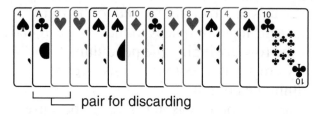

pair for discarding

Aim

To discard all the cards in adjacent pairs which add up to an even number.

Playing

● Starting at one end or the other, remove

and discard any two adjacent cards whose ranks total an even number, e.g. ace C + 3H = 1 + 3 = 4.

● After discarding the pair, close the gap in the row and see whether further play is possible at the new junction.

● Continue in this way until you have discarded the entire pack.

● If the game becomes blocked, count the number of cards remaining and aim to get a lower score next time.

● FOUR-LEAF CLOVER
An easy discard game, particularly suitable for the young player.

Cards

A standard 52-card deck from which the 10s have been removed, leaving 48 cards.

The layout

Deal 16 cards face up in four rows of four cards each. (See sample layout overleaf.)

Aim

To discard all the cards as batches of three picture (face) cards of the same suit and as batches of two or more cards of the same suit that add up to 15.

A sample layout for Four-leaf Clover

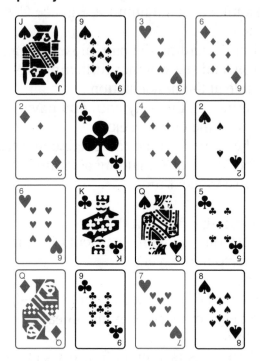

Playing
● Remove from the layout any two or more cards that are of the same suit and add up to 15. Aces are low, i.e. count as one.
● In the sample layout the ace, 5 and 9 of clubs add up to 15 and can be discarded

from the layout. Any spaces are filled using new cards from the top of the stock.

● Leave any picture cards where they are until a J, Q and K of the same suit are all showing, and then remove the three together. Continue discarding as many cards as you can, and dealing new cards to fill the gaps.

● You win when you can deal all the cards from your hand and discard all the cards from the layout.

● ONE-TO-NINE

Sometimes called Tower of Hanoi, this game is a fairly simple exercise in card shifting.

Cards

Nine cards only: ace to 9 of a chosen suit.

The layout

Shuffle the cards thoroughly before dealing them face up in three overlapping columns of three cards each. (See overleaf.)

Aim

To shift all the cards so that they are in a single column and in numerical sequence from 9 down to ace.

A sample layout for One-to-Nine

Playing

● Only exposed cards are available and only one card at a time may be moved from one column to another.

● The card that is moved must always go on a card of higher rank. For example, an 8 can be placed on a 9 but not on a 4.

● Whenever a column becomes empty, one of the two exposed cards may be placed there. Continue moving cards from one column to another in this manner until you have built the entire sequence.

● The game will come out, but it may take anywhere between a dozen or so moves, or over 100, depending on the effectiveness of your strategy and the fall of the cards. Getting the 9 and 8 in proper sequence at the top of a column is often the hardest part.

● WISH

Another simple discard game suitable for the young player. This one is a version of the simple game of Pairs. It works by chance alone.

Cards

A standard 52-card deck from which all the 2s, 3s, 4s, 5s and 6s have been removed, leaving a deck of 32 cards.

The layout

Deal eight piles of four cards each face up in a row. (See sample layout overleaf.)

Aim

To discard all the exposed cards in pairs of the same rank.

Playing

● Look at the exposed cards (those on top of the piles) and where there are two of the same rank, e.g. two 8s or two Js, discard that pair.

● Continue in this way, discarding exposed cards in pairs of the same rank (buried cards cannot be used until they are uncovered). Keep removing as many pairs as you can for as long as you can.

● If you are able to clear away all the cards you have won.

A sample layout for Wish

  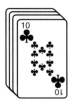 

◆ KNOCKOUT

Knockout is sometimes played with a full pack. The quick and simple version described here uses a piquet deck of 32 cards.

Cards

A standard 52-card deck from which all the 2s, 3s, 4s, 5s and 6s have been removed.

The layout

Deal a row of three cards face up.

Aim

To discard all eight cards of the chosen suit.

Playing

● The highest ranking of the three cards (aces are high) determines the suit to be discarded.

● If there are two cards of the same high rank, use the card on the left to determine the suit.

● Now discard the high card of the chosen suit, plus any other cards of that suit.

A sample layout for Knockout after the initial deal where the ace C is discarded and replaced with new card ace D

chosen suit

A sample layout after three deals

discards

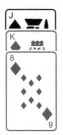

● Fill the space or spaces with new cards dealt from stock, but these cards cannot be discarded even if of the chosen suit.

● Now deal three cards face up, one on each pile.

● Discard any exposed cards of the chosen suit.

● Any spaces are now filled with cards from stock so that the layout now consists of two rows forming three columns of overlapping cards. Again, new cards cannot be discarded.

● Now deal three cards face up, one on each pile, and repeat the discard procedure as before. Two more rounds of dealing and discarding are carried out, giving five rounds in all.

● Now all the cards, except those which have been discarded, are gathered up and shuffled thoroughly, and the whole procedure with the stock is repeated as before, except that the chosen suit has already been decided. Two such redeals are allowed.

● The game is won if all eight cards of the chosen suit can be discarded.

◆ LITTLE LOTS

Little Lots, also known as Pairs, is sometimes played with a full pack. The version described here uses a piquet deck of 32 cards.

Cards

A standard 52-card deck from which all the 2s, 3s, 4s, 5s and 6s have been removed.

The layout

Deal the whole deck of 32 cards in eight piles of four cards each, face down. Then turn up the top card of each pile.

A sample layout

Aim

To discard all the cards in matching pairs.

Playing

● Discard in pairs those exposed cards that are of the same rank.

● When a card has been discarded, turn over the next card in the pile to expose it, and continue pairing and discarding as before.

● When two cards have been discarded from a pile, the two remaining cards are turned up, their order remaining the same.

● If they are a pair, they are discarded. If not, the topmost card only is available for pairing.

On average, the entire pack can be discarded about one time in six.

✘ AMAZONS

A challenging game, Amazons is played with a piquet deck from which the Ks have been removed. The Q is the highest card, hence the game's name – that of the female-led tribe, the Amazons.

Cards

A standard 52-card deck from which all the 2s, 3s, 4s, 5s, 6s and Ks have been removed.

The layout
Deal a row of four cards face up to start the reserve. Foundation aces, as they become available, are placed in a row above the reserve.

A sample layout

foundations

reserve

Aim
To build upon the foundation aces, within suit, in ascending order from 7 to Q.

Playing
● Check the reserve to see whether any aces are present. If so, move the ace or aces into position in the foundation row, filling the row from left to right.

● Deal four more cards face up, one on top of each reserve pile or space left by a moved ace.

● Again, move any aces to the foundation row and then make any possible moves following these rules.

● The top of each reserve pile is available for play only on the foundation immediately above it, except that a Q – to complete the sequence in suit – may be played from any pile.

● Continue to deal the stock in this way, four cards at a time, one on each pile, and then make whatever moves are possible.

● When the stock is exhausted, redeal by gathering the reserve piles together, each upon its left-hand neighbour.

● Then turn the pile over and without shuffling deal four new reserves. Then play as before.

● Continue redealing and playing in this manner until the game is won, or until it becomes blocked, i.e. running through two successive deals without placing a single card, in which case the game is lost.

3. Games using two decks

● BRITISH SQUARE

A classic game, related to Napoleon's Square (p.162), and with slightly unusual building on foundations. The game comes out more often than not and requires a moderately large space.

Cards

Two standard 52-card decks.

The layout

Deal four rows of four cards each, face up. Aces, one of each suit, when released during play go into a foundation row above the layout. (See sample layout overleaf.)

Aim

To build up the aces in suit to Ks, and then add the duplicate Ks and build down in suit to aces.

Playing

● Using cards from the layout, build as far as you can to foundations or to other cards in the layout. Within the layout, you can build up or down in suit, but once you have

A sample layout for British Square

foundations

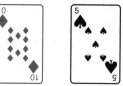

decided on a direction for a given pile, you must stick to that throughout the game.

● Only one card at a time may be moved from the top of one pile to another. One pile can be reversed on another.

● Builds on the layout cannot turn the corner but must end with an ace or K.

● When all possible moves have been made to foundations or layout, turn over one card at a time from stock to play to foundations, to the layout, or face up to a discard pile.

● Spaces in the layout may be filled from stock or from the discard pile, the top card of which is always available.

● There is no redeal.

● BUSY ACES

A straightforward building game. It comes out more often than not and requires a moderately large space.

Cards

Two standard 52-card decks.

The layout

Deal two rows of six cards, face up. Aces, as they become available, are placed in a foundation row above the layout.

Aim

To build all eight aces in suit to Ks.

Playing

● Build whatever you can to foundations and then build downwards, within suit, on cards in the layout.

● After moves have been exhausted, turn up one card at a time from stock and play to foundations, to the layout, or face up to a discard pile.

● Spaces in the layout may be filled from stock or from the discard pile, the top card of which is always available.

● There is no redeal.

A sample layout for Busy Aces

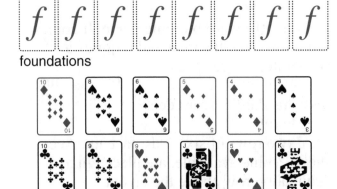

foundations

● CAPRICIEUSE

Another classic game that usually comes
out. It requires a moderately large space.

Cards

Two standard 52-card decks.

The layout

Select one ace and one K of each suit and
place them in a foundation row as shown.
Deal the rest of the pack into 12 face-up
piles, arranged in two rows of six, playing
stock cards straight to foundations where
possible (see Playing).

Aim

To build foundation aces up in suit to Ks,
and foundation Ks down in suit to aces.

Playing

● As you deal face up from stock, play onto
the foundations any card that can be built in
sequence, upwards on aces or downwards
on Ks.

● Then continue dealing as before, making
sure you place a card on each of the 12 piles
in order, without missing out any piles.

● Continue in this way until all cards are
dealt. During the deal, no cards from the
layout can be moved.

● After the stock is dealt, use exposed cards on the layout for building on foundations, upwards on aces and downwards on Ks.
● Exposed cards on the layout can be built on one another one card at a time within suit, either up or down, and even changing

A sample layout after the first deal

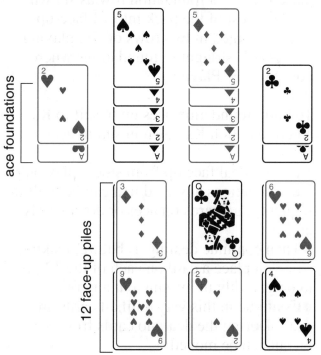

direction within a column, but without
turning the corner.

● Two redeals are allowed.

● To form the new stock, pick up the piles in
the reverse order, so that the last-dealt pile is
on top.

king foundations

● DIPLOMAT

A game that is quick to set up and comes out
more often than not. It requires a moderately
large space.

Cards

Two standard 52-card decks.

A sample layout

foundations

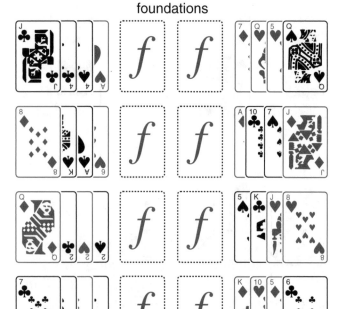

The layout

Deal two rows of four overlapping cards, side by side, leaving a space between them at least two cards wide. Continue in the same way to deal three more sets of rows. The spaces between adjacent rows will be filled with foundation aces as they become available.

Aim

To build the suits in rank order to kings, using aces as foundation cards.

Playing

● Play exposed cards from the layout to foundations where possible.

● Then make moves within the layout, building downwards on exposed cards regardless of suit.

● When moves are exhausted, turn over a card from stock and play it to the foundations, to the layout or, if unplayable, face up to a discard pile.

● The top card of the discard pile, the top card of stock and the exposed cards in the layout are all available for play and to fill any spaces that open up in the layout.

● One turn and redeal of the discard pile is allowed.

● HARP

Essentially a two-pack version of Klondike
(p.115), this game is considerably easier
than the one-pack version. It requires a
fairly large space.

Cards

Two standard 52-card decks.

The layout

Deal one card face up and eight more face
down in a row from left to right. Deal the

A sample layout

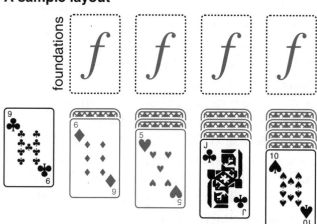

next row overlapping the first and starting
with the first card face up on the second
column and seven more face down on the
remaining columns. Continue in this way to
form nine columns with an exposed card at
the bottom of each, and with nine cards in
the final column. Aces, as they become
available, are placed in a foundation row
above the layout.

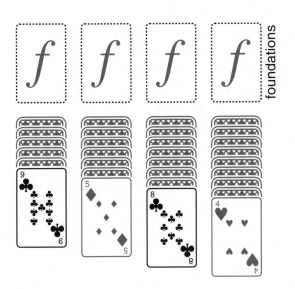

Aim

To build the suits upwards in rank order to kings, using the aces as foundation cards.

Playing

● Play one card at a time, using exposed cards from the layout or using the top card from stock. A card may be placed onto an exposed card in the columns, in alternate colours and descending numerical order.

● As a card is removed from a column, the next card is turned face up. Once the foundation aces are released during play, cards may be built onto them in suits in ascending numerical order.

● Any card from stock which cannot be played immediately is placed face up on a discard pile. The top card of this pile is always available for play.

● When a column is used up, and a space created, fill the space with an available K or with a properly built sequence with a K at its base (this is the only occasion that more than one card at a time can be moved).

● The discard pile can be turned and redealt as many times as necessary, until the game is won or there is a blockage.

● HOUSE IN THE WOOD

House in the Wood, sometimes called
Double Fan, is a two-pack version of La
Belle Lucie (p.61), but works out much
more often than the one-pack version. It
requires a large space.

Cards

Two standard 52-card decks.

The layout

Deal all the cards face up in 34 fans of three
cards each, plus a remaining fan of two
cards. The exposed card of each fan is
available for building onto foundations or
onto other exposed cards. Aces are moved to
a foundation row below the layout as they
become available. (See layout overleaf.)

Aim

To release the aces, and build them up
within suit to Ks.

Playing

● The exposed cards of the fans are available
for play to foundations, building upwards
within suit.

● Exposed cards in the layout can also be
played to one another building upwards or
downwards in suit, even reversing direction

A sample layout for House in the Wood

foundation aces

within a pile, but not turning the corner.
● Only one card at a time may be moved.
● Any spaces created by clearing away a fan
may not be filled.
● There is no redeal and the game is played
until won or until there is a blockage.
Tips
Aim to break up those fans containing two
or more cards of the same suit. Building
upwards on the layout is only a temporary
expedient. Such builds will need to be
reversed to be playable onto foundations.

● MOUNT OLYMPUS
A game which has an attractive layout. It
comes out more often than not and requires
a large amount of space.
Cards
Two standard 52-card decks.
The layout
Remove all the aces and 2s and place them,
face up, in an alternating pattern of rank and
colour exactly as shown overleaf. They
form the mount, with each ace or 2 as a
foundation card. Below the mount deal nine
cards face up to form a pyramid.

A sample layout

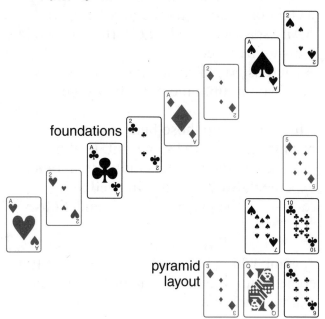

foundations

pyramid
layout

Aim

To build the foundations upwards in suit, by
2s, in the following manner. Aces are built
upon using odd numbers to form the
sequence ace, 3, 5, 7, 9, J, K; 2s are built
upon using even numbers to form the
sequence 2, 4, 6, 8, 10, Q.

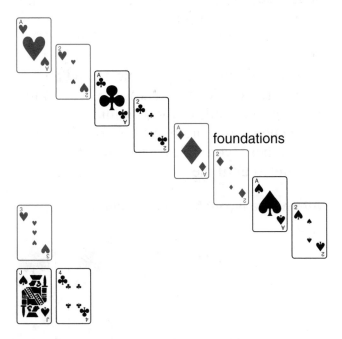

foundations

Playing

● All exposed cards in the pyramid layout
are available for play to foundations,
building upwards by 2s. They may also be
played to other exposed cards in the layout,
building downwards by 2s.

● All the cards in a layout pile, providing
they are of the appropriate suit and are all in

sequence, can be transferred as a whole and built onto another pile.

● A space in the pyramid layout is filled from stock.

● When all moves are completed and all spaces filled, nine new cards are dealt onto the exposed cards of the pyramid.

● The new cards are played to foundations, or to other layout piles. This process is continued until the stock is used up.

Alternative layout for Mount Olympus

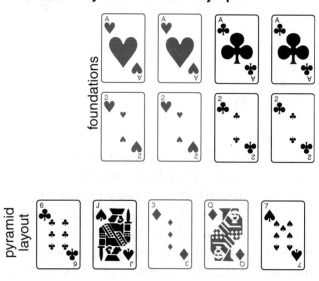

Tips

Within the layout, a high-value card dealt on top of lower rank cards will block that pile unless the card can be removed. Plan ahead to remove such potential blockages.

Alternative layout

An alternative layout may be used where space is limited. This layout, though less interesting, makes building on layout and foundations easier.

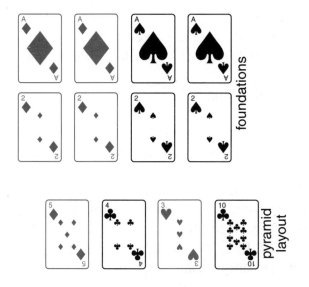

● NAPOLEON'S SQUARE

Napoleon's Square, also called Quadruple
Line, is really a simpler form of Napoleon at
St Helena (p.195). The game works out in
most instances and requires a moderately
large space.

Cards

Two standard 52-card decks.

The layout

Deal 12 piles of four cards each to form three
sides of a square as shown. The cards are
dealt one at a time to each pile in rotation,
starting at the bottom left. The aces, as they
become available, are placed in two
foundation rows in the middle of the layout.

Aim

To build the foundation aces upwards in suit
to Ks.

Playing

● Any exposed aces are moved to foundation
rows.

● Exposed cards in the layout are played
either to foundations, building upwards
within suit, or to other exposed cards in the
layout, building downwards within suit.

● Cards in appropriate sequence and suit

A sample layout

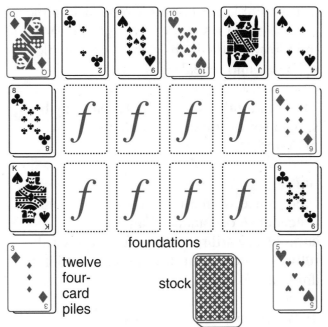

foundations

twelve four-card piles

stock

within a pile can be built as a unit upon other piles.

● When moves are exhausted, turn over one card at a time from the stock and play to foundations or layout, making moves as before.

● Unplayable cards from stock are placed face up on a discard pile.

● Spaces created in the layout are filled with any available card or built sequence in the layout, or from stock or from the discard pile, the top card of which is always available.

● There is no redeal.

Alternative play

The initial piles within the layout may be spread for examination, so aiding forward planning.

● PRECEDENCE

Precedence, sometimes called Order of Precedence or Panama Canal, has straightforward rules but often stubbornly refuses to come out. It requires a moderate amount of space.

Cards

Two standard 52-card decks.

The layout

The layout begins when the first K is dealt from stock. This is placed face up at the left end of a foundation row. The seven other foundation cards – any Q, J, 10, 9, 8, 7, 6 – are placed in their appropriate places in the foundation row as they become available. The foundations must be moved into place in the order given. For example, a foundation J cannot be placed until a foundation K and Q are in place.

A sample layout

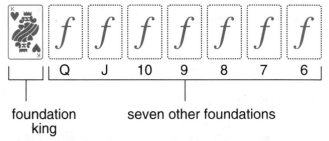

| | | | | | | |
| Q | J | 10 | 9 | 8 | 7 | 6 |

foundation   seven other foundations
king

Aim

To build downwards on foundation cards, regardless of suit, to form sequences of 13 cards, turning the corner where necessary.

Playing

● Turn over the stock, one card at a time, playing the card to foundations, building downwards on any foundation cards that are in place.

● Unplayable cards are placed face up on a discard pile, the top card of which is always available. Continue in this way until the stock is exhausted. Two redeals (without shuffling) are allowed.

● QUEEN OF ITALY

In this unusual game, sometimes called Signora or Terrace, a strategic decision has to be made at the outset. The game comes out more often than not and requires a moderately large space.

Cards

Two standard 52-card decks.

A sample layout

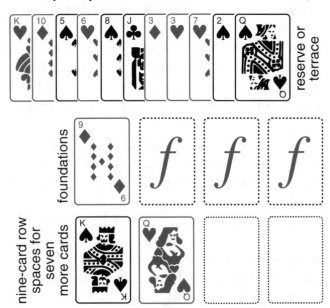

The layout

Deal 11 cards face up and overlapping in a single row. These cards form the reserve or 'terrace'. Below the terrace deal three cards face up in a row. By taking into account those cards in the reserve, choose one of these three cards to be the rank used for foundations. Move this card to form the start of a foundation row. The two other cards (unless of the same rank as the foundation) are placed at the beginning of a row below the foundation row. Seven more cards are then dealt face up to complete a bottom row of nine cards.

Aim

To build the foundation cards into eight
complete 13-card sequences, alternating in
colours, and turning the corner as
appropriate.

Playing

● At the start, it is important to choose a
suitable card as the foundation rank.

● In the reserve row, only the exposed card
is available for play at any one time. Also,
reserve cards are available only to play to
foundations. So, it makes sense not to
choose a foundation card that is of the same
rank as cards buried deeply in the reserve.

● Cards in the bottom row are available for
play. Any available cards of the same rank
as the first foundation card are placed in the
foundation row.

● Cards from the bottom row can be played
to foundations, building upwards in
alternating colours, or played to other cards
in the bottom row, building downwards in
alternating colours and turning the corner
where necessary. Only one card at a time
may be moved.

● Any spaces in the bottom row are filled

from stock or the top of the discard pile, never from cards in the layout or reserve.

● Cards in the reserve row, as they become exposed, are only playable to foundations.

● When moves are exhausted, turn over the stock one card at a time, playing to the foundations or to the bottom row.

● Unplayable cards are placed face up on the discard pile, the top card of which is always available for play. There is one redeal (without shuffling) and the game is lost if a card is unplayable during the redeal.

Tips

The strategy for the game is largely determined by the need to free all cards of the terrace (reserve) in the required order. Bear this in mind when choosing a foundation card and when building.

● SLY FOX

A game with an unusual amount of choice. Played skilfully, the game comes out more often than not. It requires plenty of time and a moderately large space.

Cards

Two standard 52-card decks.

The layout

Arrange four foundation aces – one of each
suit – vertically at the left, and four
foundation Ks – one of each suit – vertically
at the right. Between these columns deal out
four rows of five cards each. These rows
form the reserve.

A sample layout

foundations   reserve   foundations

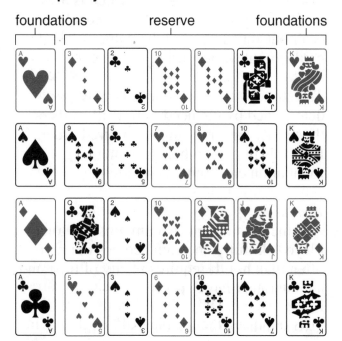

Aim

To build the foundation aces up in suit to
Ks, and the foundation Ks down in suit to
aces.

Playing

● Use cards from the reserve to build within
suit on the foundations.

● Where a space in the reserve opens up, fill
it with the top card dealt from stock.

● When moves are exhausted, turn up cards
from stock one at a time.

● Play cards to foundations where possible,
and when not, place the card on any one of
the reserve piles (this game does not use a
discard pile), thinking ahead as to how you
will use these cards later.

● Continue from stock, playing to
foundations where you can and when you
cannot, playing to the reserve piles.

● Keep a running total of the number of
cards you have played to the reserve. When
you reach 20, stop.

● Now try to make any new plays that have
become possible as a result of adding cards
to the reserve. Only the top cards of reserve
piles are available for play, although playing

the top card releases the one below. When moves are made to foundations, any spaces created in the reserve no longer have to be filled immediately. They may be filled from stock, either now or later.

● When all moves are complete, play from stock onto foundations, onto reserve piles or into spaces. Again, when 20 cards have been added to the reserve, stop and try to move exposed cards from the reserve to foundations.

● Continue in this way until the stock is exhausted (the last deal may well have less than 20 cards).

● There is no redeal, and cards need to be thoughtfully placed in the reserve if the game is to come out.

Tips

Reserve piles can be used for building within suit in ascending or descending order. If you do this, make sure that duplicate cards are built in separate piles and in opposite directions. You may wish to earmark one or two reserve piles for the four aces and four Ks and the four 2s and four Qs that you will need to complete the final sequences.

● ST HELENA

Not to be confused with Napoleon at St
Helena (p.195), this game is sometimes
called Napoleon's Favourite or
Washington's Favourite and has some
unusual features. The game comes out more
often than not and requires a moderately
large space.

Cards

Two standard 52-card decks.

The layout

Remove one ace and one K of each suit and
place the Ks face up in a first row and the
aces in a second row. These are the
foundations. Now deal out the rest of the
pack clockwise in 12 piles around the
foundations: four cards on top, two on the
right side, four below, and two on the left.
Keep dealing, one card on each of the 12
piles, until all the cards are dealt. (See
sample layout overleaf.)

Aim

To build the foundation aces up in suit to
Ks, and the foundation Ks down in suit to
aces.

A sample layout

foundations

Playing
● In the first deal, exposed cards on piles can be played to foundations, or to other piles, but there are some unusual rules.
● Only exposed cards in the top row of the layout can be played to foundation Ks.
● Similarly, only exposed cards in the

bottom row can be played to foundation aces.

● Exposed cards at the sides of the layout can, however, be placed on either foundation row.

● Building on the foundation aces is upwards within suit; on the foundation Ks it is downwards within suit. Building on the cards around the layout is upwards or downwards, regardless of suit or colour, and the direction may be reversed within a pile.

● Only one card at a time can be moved, and there is no turning the corner.

● When all moves are exhausted, the deal is over.

● Two redeals are allowed.

● To form the new stock, pick up the twelve piles in the reverse order in which they were dealt, i.e. anticlockwise starting at the top left-hand side.

● The last-dealt pile will be at the top when the stock is turned face down. The stock is then dealt clockwise to form 12 piles as before.

● For the redeals, the special rules no longer apply. Any card of the correct suit and rank can go on any foundation.

● SULTAN OF TURKEY

Sometimes called Emperor of Germany or simply Sultan, the game has an attractive layout. It works out more often than not and requires a moderate amount of space.

Cards

Two standard 52-card decks.

The layout

The eight Ks and an ace of hearts are placed in three rows of three, with a KH (the 'Sultan') in the central location and the ace below it. The ace and all the Ks (except the sultan) will form the foundations. A column of four cards is dealt on either side of the foundations. These columns form the reserve.

Aim

To build upwards on the foundation Ks in suit to Qs, turning the corner as required, and to build on the foundation ace in suit to Q.

Playing

● All reserve cards are available for play to foundations, building upwards in suit.

● A space in the reserve must be filled at once from the top of the discard pile, or if there is no pile, from stock.

● When all moves are exhausted, turn up the

top card from stock and play to foundations
(there is no building on the reserve) or if the
card is unplayable, place it face up on the

A sample layout

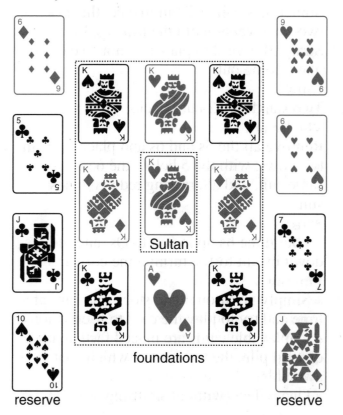

foundations

reserve   reserve

discard pile. The top of the discard pile is always available.

● Two redeals (with shuffling) are allowed.

◆ COTILLION

Sometimes called Contradance, this is a two-pack version of Quadrille (p.38). Straightforward to play, it is not so easy to make come out.

Cards

Two standard 52-card decks.

The layout

Remove all the 5s and 6s and place them in two rows, with the 5 below the 6 of the same suit, and alternating red and black suits.

Aim

To build the 6s up in suit to Qs, and the 5s down in suit to Ks, turning the corner.

Playing

● Simply go through the stock one card at a time and try to play the card to foundations.

● Unplayable cards are placed face up on a discard pile, the top card of which is always available.

● One redeal (without shuffling) is allowed.

A sample layout for Cotillion

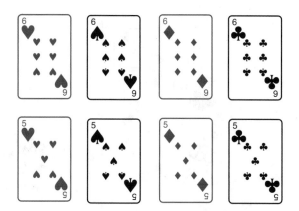

◆ CRAZY QUILT

A fascinating game requiring thought and
skill, it is also known as Japanese Rug or
Indian Carpet. The names reflect the
interesting layout.

Cards

Two standard 52-card decks.

The layout

Eight foundation cards are laid in a row by
selecting an ace and a K from each suit. In
the space above the foundations, eight rows
of eight cards each are dealt face up from
the stock. Alternate cards are placed on their

A sample layout

reserve 'quilt'

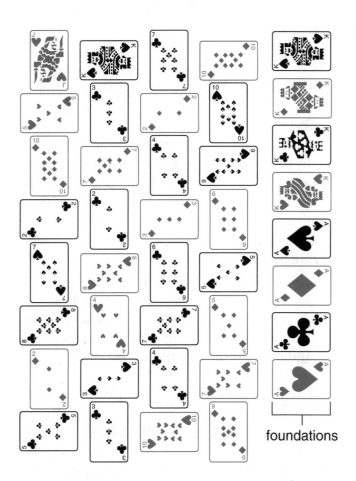

foundations

sides, forming a quilt pattern. These 64 cards are the reserve, and the remaining cards form the stock.

Aim

To build in suits, upwards on foundation aces to Ks, and downwards on foundation Ks to aces.

Playing

● A card can be removed from the reserve onto a foundation providing at least one of its narrow edges is free. Thus, any of the 16 cards that project from the four sides of the quilt are immediately available. Removing one of these cards makes one or more cards available for play.

● Spaces in the reserve remain empty.

● After available cards have been played from the reserve, one card is turned up from the stock and is used either to build on the foundations or is placed face up on the discard pile.

● The top card on the discard pile is always available for play.

● Providing there is already at least one card on the discard pile, available cards of the same suit from the reserve can be added to it

in ascending or descending order. This rule
can allow the release of a useful card from
inside the quilt that does not have a narrow
edge free.

● If required, the stock can be shuffled and
redealt once.

Tips

If duplicate cards are both buried deep in the
layout, it is usually advisable to free one of
these as soon as you can.

◆ CRESCENT

Its title is obvious once you see the layout
(overleaf). The game usually comes out if
played skilfully. It requires a moderately
large amount of space.

Cards

Two standard 52-card decks.

The layout

Remove one ace and one K of each suit and
place these in two rows, with each ace above
the K of the same suit. Then deal the rest of
the cards in 16 piles of six cards each, with
the first five in each pile face down and the
final card face up. The 16 piles are arranged
in a semicircle enclosing the foundation rows.

Aim

To build the foundation aces upwards in suit
to Ks, and the foundation Ks downwards in
suit to aces.

Playing

● The top card of each pile is available for
play to foundations, building upwards in suit

A sample layout

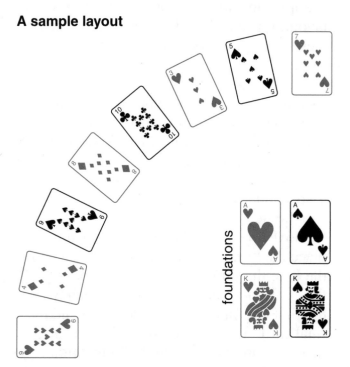

foundations

on the aces and building downwards in suit
on the Ks.

● As the top card in a pile is played, it
releases the next card below.

● Exposed cards within the crescent can also
be played to one another, one card at a time,
building upwards or downwards in suit, and

foundations

turning the corner or even reversing
direction within the same pile.

● Spaces created by clearing away entire
piles are not filled.

● When two foundation sequences of the
same suit meet, the top cards being
consecutive in sequence, any or all cards of
one pile may be reversed upon the other,
except the ace or K at the bottom.

● There is an unusual rule. When moves are
exhausted, a shift is allowed. This involves
taking the bottom card of each crescent pile
and bringing it to the top, turning it face up.
This must be done for *all* crescent piles,
including those piles where there are
sequences and no face-down cards. Thus
shifting, although creating new
opportunities, also disrupts some of the
work already done.

● Up to three shifts are allowed in a game.

Tips

When two foundation sequences meet, hold
them intact in case you wish to use the
reversal privilege to help extract buried
cards from crescent piles later in the game.
Avoid changing the direction of build on a

pile unless you can see a way of later splitting the build into two one-way sequences.

◆ FROG

Also known as Toad-in-the-hole or simply Toad, this game uses eight aces as foundations.

Cards

Two standard 52-card decks.

The layout

A reserve of 13 cards is dealt face up. Any aces among these are laid out as foundations and cards are added to the reserve to make up 13 cards. If an ace does not appear, one is found from the stock and placed in position. The remaining seven aces will be laid out as foundations as they appear during play. Space will also be required for five discard piles. (See sample layout overleaf.)

Aim

To build numerically upwards within suit, from 2 to K, on the eight foundations. The game is complete when the top card of each foundation pile is a K.

Playing

● One card at a time is turned up from the
stock and added to a foundation or placed on
one of up to five discard piles.

● Cards can be added to any discard pile.
The exposed card of each is always
available for play.

● It is useful to keep one discard pile for,
say, high-value cards. Cards should be
added to discard piles in reverse numerical
order – for example, 10, 9, 8 rather than 8,
9, 10 – to avoid burying the lower-ranking
cards that will be needed first.

● Spaces in the row of discard piles are
filled from the stock.

● The exposed card of the reserve is always
available for play.

● When the reserve runs out, it is not
replaced.

A sample layout

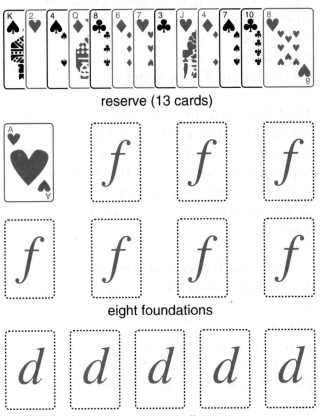

reserve (13 cards)

eight foundations

five discard piles

◆ GRAND DUCHESS

This old and venerable game comes out
more often than not. It requires a moderately
large space.

Cards

Two standard 52-card decks.

The layout

Deal four cards in a row face up to start the
layout. Deal two cards face down in a pile to
start the reserve. Two foundation rows at the
top of the layout will be filled with an ace
and a K of each suit, as they become
available. An ace is placed above a K of the
same suit.

Aim

To build the foundation aces up in suit to
Ks, and the foundation Ks down in suit to
aces.

Playing

● Make any moves to foundations. Then
deal four more cards to the bottom row, so
covering the existing cards and filling any
spaces.

● At the same time deal two more cards face
down to the reserve pile.

● Try to make moves from the bottom row

A sample layout

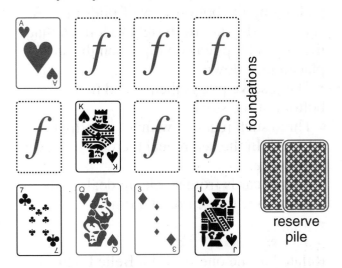

to foundations, the top card of each pile
being available.

● Continue in this way, making whatever
moves you can, and then dealing four cards
face up and two face down for the next play.

● When the stock is used up, turn over the
reserve pile and spread it out in a fan, all the
cards of which are available.

● From the fan play whatever cards you can
to foundations, adding exposed cards from
the bottom row where you can. When moves

are exhausted, form the new stock by picking up the bottom row of piles in reverse order, i.e. from right to left, so that the last-dealt pile is on top when the stock is placed face down.

● The reserve pile is then added to the bottom of the stock.

● Three such redeals (without shuffling) are allowed. In the last redeal there is, however, no reserve.

● All the cards from stock are dealt to the bottom row, four cards at a time.

◆ INTELLIGENCE

Related to the one-deck La Belle Lucie (p.61) and the two-deck House in the Wood (p.155), Intelligence is harder than both. Skilfully played, the game comes out about one time in five or six. It requires a moderately large space.

Cards

Two standard 52-card decks.

The layout

Deal out 18 fans of three cards each as shown. During the deal, if aces appear, place them in an appropriate position in the

foundation row above the layout. Deal the
next card as their replacement in the layout.

A sample layout

foundations

The remaining cards form the stock.

Aim

To build the foundation aces up in suit to Ks.

Playing

● Exposed cards of the fans are available to be played on foundations, building upwards within suit.

● Alternatively, exposed cards may be played to one another, one card at a time, building upwards or downwards in suit.

● Within a pile, sequence may be reversed if required.

● A space made by clearing away an entire fan is filled by dealing a new fan of three cards from stock.

● Aces buried in the fan are not immediately released when dealt in this way. Incidentally, clearing away fans is the only way that new cards from stock can be brought into play. Two redeals (with shuffling) are allowed.

● If the game blocks, or when no cards remain in stock, gather all the fans together and shuffle them with any remaining stock.

● When redealing, any aces that appear are placed directly in the foundation row, as in the original deal. Continue as before.

◆ NAPOLEON AT ST HELENA

Also known as Big Forty and Forty Thieves, this is one of many patience games that may have been played by Napoleon.

Cards

Two standard 52-card decks.

The layout

Ten cards are dealt face up in a row. Three more rows of ten cards are dealt, each overlapping the last, making ten columns of four overlapping cards. Space will be needed for eight foundations and a discard pile. (See sample layout overleaf.)

Aim

To build upwards from ace to K, in suits, on eight foundation spaces, playing all cards.

Playing

● As aces become available they are placed on the foundation spaces.

● The exposed card of each column is available and may be played either onto a foundation, building upwards within suit, or onto another column, building downwards within suit.

● Alternatively, a card may be turned up from stock. If it cannot be used it is placed face up on the discard pile, and remains available for play until another card is put on top of it (overlapping, so that the ones beneath are visible).

A sample layout

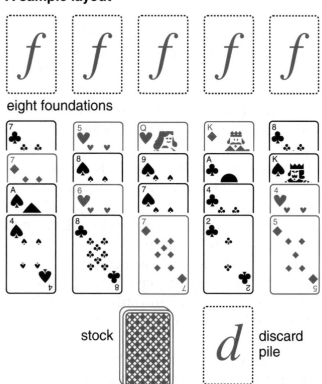

● When a column disappears a new column is begun with any available card. It is best to choose this card with care, keeping in mind its usefulness for bringing others into play.

● There is no redeal.

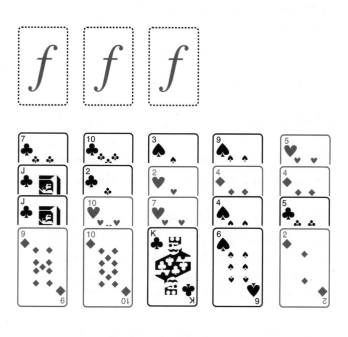

◆ ODD AND EVEN

One of several games, such as Royal
Cotillion (p.200) and Royal Rendezvous
(p.202), where even-numbered cards are
built on one foundation and odd numbers
are built on another. The game comes out
about once or twice in ten attempts and
requires a moderately large space.

Cards

Two standard 52-card decks.

The layout

Deal three rows of three cards each face up.
These form the reserve. Four aces and 2s, as
they become available, are moved into a
foundation row or rows above the reserve.

Aim

To build the foundation aces up in suit by
twos through to Qs, i.e. ace, 3, 5, 7, 9, J, K,
2, 4, 6, 8, 10, Q. To build foundation 2s up
in suit by twos, through to Ks, i.e. 2, 4, 6, 8,
10, Q, ace, 3, 5, 7, 9, J, K.

Playing

● All reserve cards are available to play to
foundations. When a space in the reserve
opens up it is filled at once from the discard
pile, or, if there is none, from the stock.

● Turn up cards from stock one at a time,
putting unplayable cards in a discard pile.
The top card of this is always available.
● One redeal (without shuffling) is allowed.

A sample layout

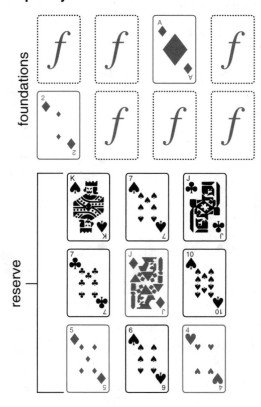

◆ ROYAL COTILLION

This game, related to Odd and Even (p.198), takes its name from an 18th-century dance that was performed at the French court.

Cards

Two standard 52-card decks.

A sample layout

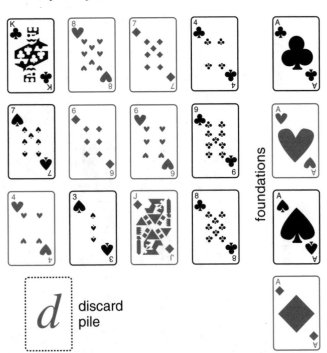

The layout

Find an ace and a 2 of each suit and place
them centrally in two columns, aces on the
left. These eight cards are the foundations.
Some players prefer to lay down the aces
and 2s as they become available during play.

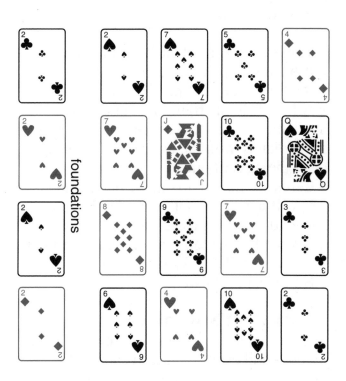

Twelve cards are dealt face up, in three rows
of four cards, to the left of the top three
aces; and 16 cards, in four rows of four
cards, are dealt to the right of the 2s.

Aim

To build in suits on the foundations. On
aces: 3, 5, 7, 9, J, K, 2, 4, 6, 8, 10, Q, and
on 2s: 4, 6, 8, 10, Q, ace, 3, 5, 7, 9, J, K.

Playing

● The bottom card of each column in the
left-hand group is available for play.

● Spaces created are not filled in this group.

● All cards in the right-hand group are
available for play and spaces must be filled
immediately with the top card of the stock
or of the discard pile.

● Cards are turned up one by one from the
stock. If a card cannot be used to build on
foundations, it is placed face up on the
discard pile. The top card of the discard pile
is always available for play.

● No redeal is allowed.

◆ **ROYAL RENDEZVOUS**

Another interesting game where building is
by odd- and even-numbered cards. The

game comes out more often than not. It
requires a moderately large space.

Cards

Two standard 52-card decks.

The layout

Remove the eight aces and place these in
two rows, with those of the same suit one
above the other. Then take four 2s of
different suits and place two on either side
of the lower row of aces. The aces and 2s
are foundations. Underneath the foundation
rows deal out two rows of eight cards each
face up. These cards are the reserve.

Four Ks – two at either end of the top
foundation row – will be added late in the
game. (See sample layout overleaf.)

Aim

To build the top row of foundation aces up
in suit to Qs, to build the lower row of aces
up in suit by odd numbers to Ks – A, 3, 5, 7,
9, J, K – and to build the 2s up in suit by
even numbers to Qs – 2, 4, 6, 8, 10, Q. The
four remaining Ks are put at either end of
the top foundation row, but only after their
couterparts have been incorporated in the
lower foundation row.

A sample layout

king foundations

foundations

reserve

foundations

king foundations

reserve

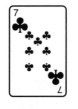  

Playing

● Cards in the two bottom rows (the reserve) are available to play to foundations.

● Spaces in the reserve must be filled at once from the discard pile or if there is none, from stock.

● Turn up cards from the stock one at a time, putting unplayable cards face up on the discard pile. The top card of this is always available.

● There is no redeal.

◆ TOURNAMENT

A game with unusual rules and interesting terminology.

Cards

Two standard 52-card decks.

The layout

Deal two columns of four cards each face up at either side of the layout. These eight cards are the 'kibitzers' (reserve). If no aces or Ks appear among them, pick up the cards, place them back in the pack, and shuffle and deal again. The game can only begin if an ace or K is present among the kibitzers.

Next, between the two columns of kibitzers

deal a row of six cards face up, and upon
these add three further rows of six cards
forming six columns of four overlapping
cards. These cards are the 'dormitzers'.
Ks and aces, as they become available, go in
two foundation rows above the dormitzers,
with the ace of a given suit above the K of
the same suit. (See sample layout overleaf.)

Aim

To build the foundation aces up in suit to Ks
and the foundation Ks down in suit to aces.

Playing

Make whatever moves you can. All kibitzers
and exposed cards of the dormitzers are
available for playing onto the foundations.

● A column space in the dormitzers must be
filled straight away with four cards from
stock.

● A space in the kibitzers may be filled by
any available card from the dormitzers, but
this can be delayed and done whenever you
wish.

● When all moves are exhausted, deal
another four rows of cards on the existing
dormitzers.

● Continue playing and dealing in this

A sample layout

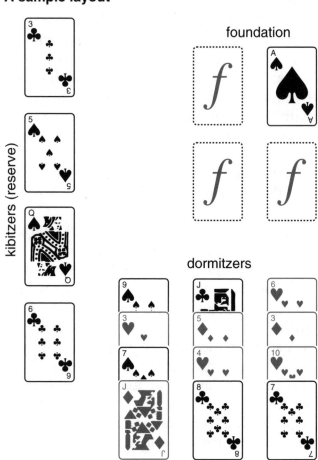

kibitzers (reserve)

foundation

dormitzers

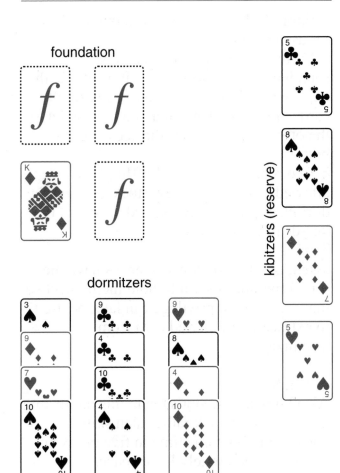

foundation

dormitzers

kibitzers (reserve)

fashion. If the stock cards run out, deal as
far as you can.

● There is a special rule. When two
foundation sequences of a suit meet, i.e. the
exposed cards are in sequence, any or all
cards of one sequence may be reversed upon
the other. This includes the ace or K at the
bottom.

● Two redeals (without shuffling) are
allowed. To form the new stock, pick up the
dormitzer piles in reverse order, so that the
last-dealt is face down.

Tips

When two foundation sequences have met,
it is sometimes useful to hold them intact so
that the reversal privilege can later be used
to extract a vital buried card from a
dormitzer.

◆ WEAVERS

Also known as Leoni's Own, this interesting
game is one of luck rather than skill. It
comes out about one time in five or six and
requires a moderately large space.

Cards

Two standard 52-card decks.

The layout

Take out one ace and K of each suit and place them in two foundation rows, with the ace above the K of the same suit. Deal the rest of the pack face up to 13 piles arranged as shown overleaf. As you deal, count the first pile as ace, the second as two, the third as three, and so on, through to K as the thirteenth pile. If the dealt card corresponds to the name (rank) of that pile, the card is an 'exile' and is placed face down in a pile to one side.

Do not miss a pile in dealing, but when a card is exiled, replace it with the next dealt card, and repeat the name of the pile as before. Continue in this way until all the cards are dealt. (See layout overleaf.)

Aim

To build the foundation aces up in suit to Ks, and the foundation Ks down in suit to aces.

Playing

● After the deal is complete, spread the cards of the 13 or K pile. All the cards of this pile, including any cards added later, are available for play to foundations.

A sample layout

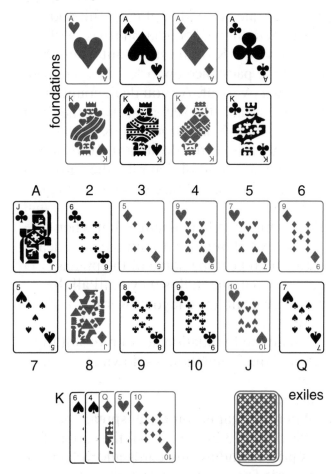

● Also available are the exposed top cards of the other piles.

● Play whatever cards you can to foundations, building upwards in suit on aces, and building downwards in suit on Ks.

● Whenever moves are exhausted, turn up the top card of the exile pile.

● If this card is playable on a foundation, you must play it. If it is unplayable, put it at the bottom of the pile that corresponds to its own rank.

● Then remove the top card of that pile and put it at the bottom of the pile of its own rank, and so on.

● Continue shifting cards in this way until a playable card is revealed on top of a pile. After putting the card just removed under its proper pile, play the revealed card to a foundation. Then make any additional moves which are opened up.

● When a K is turned up, whether during shifting or from the exile pile, it stops play.

● Put the K under the 13 pile and turn up the next exile.

● When two foundation sequences of the same suit meet, the top cards being consecutive, any or all of the cards of one pile may be reversed on the other, except for the ace or K at the bottom.

● Two redeals (without shuffling) are allowed.

● To form the new stock, gather the cards up in reverse order, beginning with the Ks pile and finishing with the aces pile, so that the Ks pile is on top and the aces pile at the bottom.

● Any unused exiles are then put at the bottom, below the aces pile.

◆ WINDMILL

Sometimes known as Propeller, this challenging game has a layout resembling propeller blades or the sails of a windmill.

Cards

Two standard 52-card decks.

The layout

Any K is placed face up in the centre as the first foundation. A reserve of eight cards is dealt face up, two on each side of the K, to represent the sails. Four foundation aces, as they become available, are placed between the sails.

A sample layout

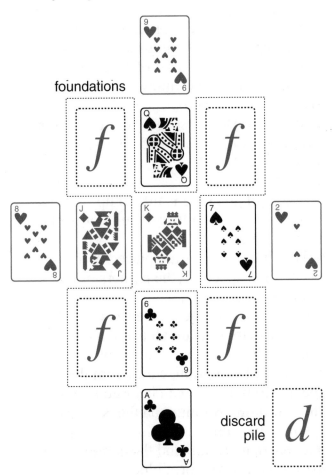

foundations

discard pile

Aim

There are two aims:

1 to build on the central K, in descending
order, regardless of colour or suit. The
sequence should consist of 13 cards from K
to ace repeated four times to make a total
sequence of 52 cards; and

2 to build on the first four aces that become
available in ascending order to K, regardless
of suit or colour.

Playing

● One card at a time is turned up from the
stock and is used either to build or is placed
on the discard pile.

● The first four aces are placed in the
foundation spaces in the corners of the
'sails'.

● Cards from the stock, the sails and the top
of the discard pile are all available for play
onto the four ace foundations and the
central K. In addition, cards from the top of
the ace foundations can be used to build on
the central K. Building on the K helps to
resolve the game.

● There is no redeal and the game is played
until it is resolved or it blocks.

● A space in the layout of the windmill sails need not be filled immediately. It can only be filled by a card from the top of the stock or the discard pile.

● Waiting to fill the space until a useful card appears enhances the chance of success.

Alternative sequences

The central card can be an ace instead of a K, in which case the four other foundations will be Ks. Sequences will then be built upwards on the central ace and downwards on the four Ks.

✂ BRAID

Also known as Plait, the game has a layout that takes the form of a braid or plait.

Cards

Two standard 52-card decks.

The layout

Twenty cards are dealt left and right diagonally, face up, overlapping as in a braid. Six cards are dealt face up in two columns either side of the braid. These columns are the reserve.

The next card is placed face up to one side of the reserve columns as the first foundation card; spaces are needed for seven more (which must be of the same rank as the first) and for a discard pile, as shown in the sample layout. The remaining stock of cards is retained for use.

Aim

To build two numerical sequences in each of the four suits, building upwards from the rank of the first foundation card and turning the corner where necessary.

Playing

● In the sample layout, the first foundation is 8D, so all the other seven foundation cards must be 8s.

A sample layout

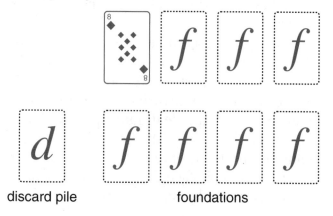

discard pile   foundations

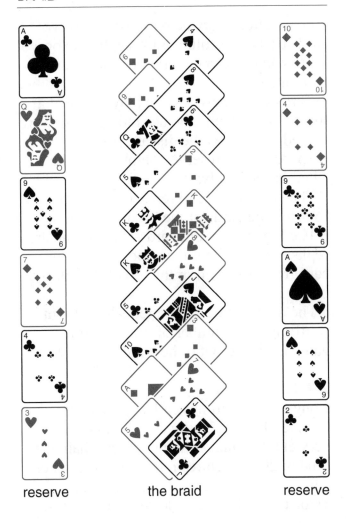

reserve   the braid   reserve

- Foundations may be built using reserve cards (from the columns), using the exposed bottom card from the braid or using cards from the stock.
- Cards from the stock are played one at a time. If they cannot be used to build they are placed face up on the discard pile.
- Spaces in the reserve columns must be filled immediately.
- The stock is used to replace any of the four middle cards of the reserve columns.
- The top and bottom cards of a column are replaced with either the exposed bottom card from the braid or the top of the discard pile.
- The discard pile can be redealt (without shuffling) any number of times until the game is played out or becomes blocked.

✖ CONGRESS

Congress, sometimes called President's Cabinet, has straightforward rules but is very challenging, coming out less than one time in 20. It requires relatively little space.

Cards

Two standard 52-card decks.

A sample layout

foundation

The layout

Deal eight cards in two columns of four each, leaving room in between for two more columns. Foundation aces, as they appear during play, are placed in these two middle columns.

Aim

To build the foundation aces up in suit to Ks.

Playing

● First, make whatever moves you can from outer columns to foundations, building up in suit.

● Cards can also be played from one outer column pile to another, one card at a time, building down regardless of suit.

● Any spaces in the outer columns are filled at once from stock, or from the discard pile, if there is one.

● When moves are exhausted, turn up cards from stock, playing either to foundations or outer columns.

● Unplayable cards are placed face up in a discard pile, the top card of which is always available.

● There is no redeal.

Tips
It pays to create spaces when there is a top
card from the discard pile worth saving.

✘ EIGHT KINGS
An unusual patience game, requiring some
ability at mental arithmetic, in which the
cards are not neatly ordered at the end of the
game. Playing Eight Kings is one way of
helping to thoroughly mix two decks.

Cards

Two standard 52-card decks

The layout

Deal eight cards face up in a row. If any of
these cards are of the same rank, e.g. two 4s,
remove the duplicate and deal a card in its
place. If any of the cards are Ks, remove
them and replace them with a newly dealt
card. Continue in this way, until you are left
with eight face-up cards, each of different
rank, and none of which are Ks. Shuffle the
removed cards back into the pack. Now deal
the remainder of the pack up into eight piles,
to form a second row below the first. Each
pile should contain 12 cards.
Each card in the top row of the layout is a

**A sample layout
during play**

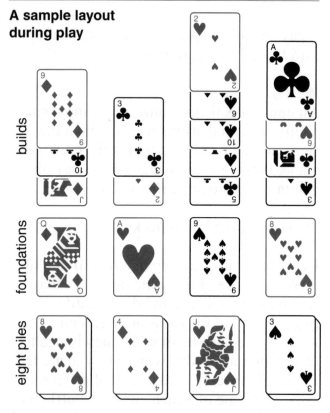

builds

foundations

eight piles

foundation card and also determines how the
sequence above it will be built.
Aim
To build up each foundation, irrespective of
colour or suit, to K. The rank of the

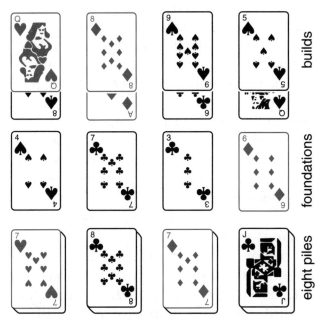

builds

foundations

eight piles

foundation card indicates how the sequence should be built. For example, a 2 is built upon in steps of two: 4, 6, 8, 10, Q, ace, 3, 5, 7, 9, J, K. Notice that this gives a sequence of 13 cards, from 2 to K, and that when you turn the corner by going above 13, the rank of the next card is found by subtracting 13, e.g. the Q is followed by an ace because $12 + 2 = 14$ and $14 - 13 = 1$. The foundation 8 is built upon in steps of eight: 8, 3, J, 6, ace, 9, 4, Q, 7, 2, 10, 5, K.

Whatever the foundation card, and therefore the interval within the sequence, the correct sequence of 13 cards will always end on a K.

Playing

● The eight exposed cards of the bottom row are available for building on foundations in accordance with the required sequence in each case. As a card is played, it exposes the card underneath.

● When moves are exhausted, or when you wish to stop play temporarily, take up the first pile of the bottom row, and deal it to the bottom row, starting at the first position (now a vacated space), and then to the second pile, the third, and so on, until the cards are all dealt. Then continue play as before.

● When play again becomes blocked, or you wish to temporarily stop play, deal out the second pile in the same manner, to the first pile (or space), the second, and so on.

● Continue in this way until you have dealt out all eight piles, after which there are no more redeals.

✘ MISS MILLIGAN

A perennially popular and challenging game using eight foundations.

Cards

Two standard 52-card decks.

The layout

Space will be needed for eight foundations. The game begins by dealing a card face up below each foundation space. This forms the first row of cards. The stock of cards is held face down in the hand. (See layout overleaf.)

Aim

As aces appear during play they are placed on the foundation spaces. The aim is then to build upwards on each ace in suit to K.

Playing

● Any aces from the first row are moved onto the foundation spaces.

● Other cards from the first row can then be built either on an ace in ascending suit sequence or onto another first-row card in alternate colours in descending sequence,

A sample layout

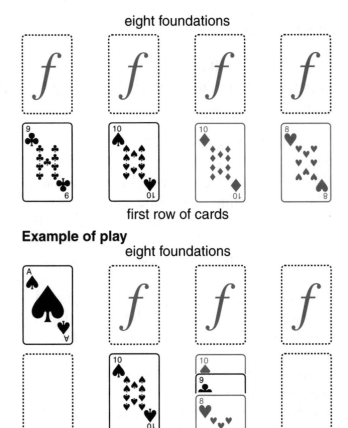

eight foundations

first row of cards

Example of play

eight foundations

first row with transfers
ready for second deal

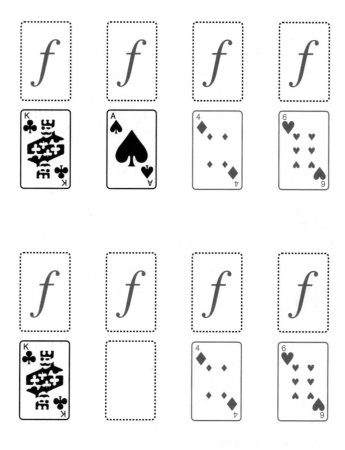

e.g. red 10, black 9, red 8 and so on.

● A second row is dealt overlapping the first row and filling empty spaces.

● Cards may then be moved onto foundation aces or onto other columns as before.

● Two or more cards can be moved together if they are in correct sequence. Spaces made from this point onwards may only be filled by a K, together with any cards already built on it. Cards continue to be dealt onto the columns and moved as before.

● It is best to take all possible moves before making the next deal.

● When the stock is used up, any single card, or sequence of cards, from one column may be lifted and used as a reserve.

● All the cards in the reserve are available to build on foundations or other columns. This is known as weaving.

● If all the cards in the reserve are used up to build, the weaving process can be repeated. However, if any card in the reserve cannot be used, the game is lost.

● Weaving can be repeated until the aim of the game is achieved or, as often happens, the game becomes blocked.

✂ ROBIN POST

An intriguing game which requires considerable spatial ability. Played very skilfully, it comes out more often than not. It has an attractive layout that requires plenty of space.

Cards

Two standard 52-card decks.

The layout

Deal 52 cards face up in nine rows forming a hexagonal array as shown overleaf. The rows, from top to bottom, contain the following numbers of cards: 4, 5, 6, 7, 8, 7, 6, 5, 4. The layout is a 'chequerboard' pattern with a card-width space between one card and the next. Four foundation aces and Ks, as they become available during play, are placed in rows below the layout.

Aim

To build the foundation aces up in suit to Ks and to build foundation Ks down in suit to aces.

Playing

● Cards in the layout are available for play when they have at least one free corner (a corner which is not touching another card or

A sample layout

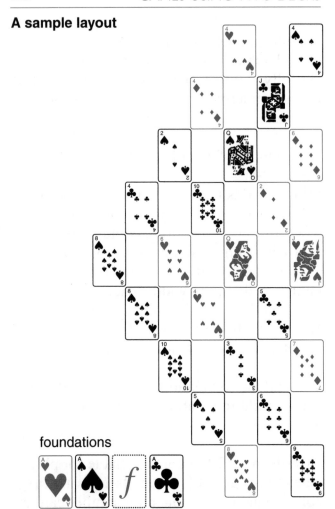

foundations

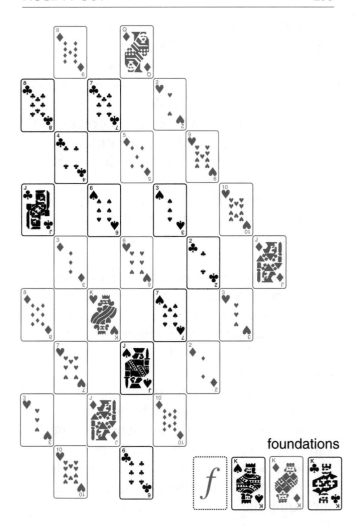

foundations

pile). These cards however cannot necessarily be moved. Those cards with two corners free can be moved. To begin, therefore, only those cards at the edge of the layout are available for play.

● A card with two or more free corners may be played to the foundations, building up within suit on aces or building down within suit on Ks.

● Alternatively, the card may be played to other 'free' cards in the layout, building in ascending or descending order and using alternate colours.

● Within a pile a sequence, once established, cannot be reversed in direction. A sequence or part-sequence can, however, be moved as a unit from one pile to another, or reversed, card by card, onto another pile, provided, of course, a proper sequence is maintained.

● A card with only one free corner may not be moved, but is available to be built upon.

● When two foundation sequences of the same suit meet, the top cards being consecutive in sequence, any or all cards of one pile may be reversed upon the other, including the ace or K at the bottom. This can provide an opportunity to remove problem blockages in the layout.

● One redeal is allowed.

● When moves are exhausted, deal out the second 52 cards, face up, in the same positions as in the first deal. Some cards will be dealt into vacated spaces, while others will be placed on top of an existing card or pile.

● Then continue playing as before until the game comes out or until you are blocked and the game is lost.

✖ SPIDER

A game in which foundations remain in the layout until building is completed. Spider has many variations. This one is said to have been popular with Franklin D. Roosevelt when he was president of the USA, and some call it the king of patience games.

Cards

Two standard 52-card decks.

The layout

Deal ten cards face down in a row. Deal two more rows face down, each overlapping the previous row. Finally deal a fourth row of

A sample layout

face-up cards. The remaining cards are kept,
face down, as the stock.

The eight Ks, as they become available, are
the foundation cards and remain in the
layout.

Aim

To build on the Ks in suits in descending
order down to ace and discard each
completed sequence until the table is
cleared.

Playing

● All ten cards at the foot of the columns are
available for play. Any of these cards may
be built onto another in descending rank

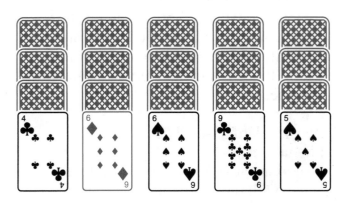

order, regardless of suit or colour.
● A sequence of cards may be moved to join
other cards in sequence.
● Nothing can be built onto an ace.
● When a face-down card is exposed, it is
turned face up and is available for play.
● Any spaces may be filled by any available
card or by a K with any cards below it.
● When no more moves are possible, ten
more cards are dealt face up from the stock
onto the foot of each column.
● Play continues as before. The final deal of
four cards is onto the four left-hand
columns.

✖ THREE PYRAMIDS

Sometimes called simply Pyramids, this challenging game has periods of relative inactivity interspersed with bouts of fast action. It needs a moderately large amount of space.

Cards

Two standard 52-card decks.

The layout

Deal nine cards face up in a 'pyramid' shape, with one card in the top row, three in the middle, and five at the bottom. The top four cards form the reserve; the bottom five form the working area where building will take place. Foundation aces and foundation Ks, one of each suit, as they become available during play, are placed in smaller pyramids at either side of the main pyramid. (See sample layout overleaf.)

Aim

To build the foundation aces up in suit to Ks and the foundation Ks down in suit to aces.

Playing

● Exposed cards in the bottom row are available to play to foundations, or for building on one another, in ascending or descending order, within suit.

● Within a pile, changing direction is not allowed, nor is turning the corner.

● Only one card may be moved at a time.

● The four cards of the reserve are available only for play to foundations, and then only when released by the play of a card below. For example, in the sample layout shown, the 5H is released for play only when the QD or the JH is played, leaving a space below the 5H. The 3C becomes available when the 6S is played. The 8D becomes available when the 4C or the 7C is moved. The 7H at the top of the pyramid becomes available when the 3C is moved.

● All spaces within the pyramid (both the reserve and the bottom row) must, at the end of the series of moves that created them, be filled from cards at the top of discard piles, or if there are no such piles, using cards from stock.

● Carefully choosing which exposed card of a discard pile will be played to which part of the main pyramid is an important part of the game's strategy.

● Make any opening moves that may be

A sample layout

reserve

spaces for foundation
kings

five cards available
for building

three discard piles

possible, and then fill any spaces with cards
from stock.

● Continue by turning up cards from stock,
three at a time, and placing them in three

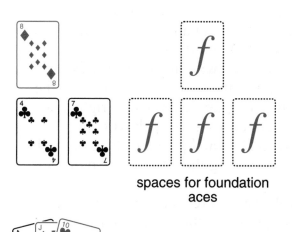

spaces for foundation
aces

discard piles from left to right.
● The top card of every discard pile is
available for play to foundations, or to
exposed cards in the bottom row.

● When the top card of a discard pile is
played, it makes available the next card.
● When moves are exhausted, deal the next
three batches of three cards onto the existing
discard piles and continue play as before.
● Carry on playing and dealing in this way
until the stock is exhausted.
● Two redeals (without shuffling) are
allowed. For the first redeal, gather up the
three discard piles, from left to right, and
form them into a new stock without
shuffling. Deal and play the stock again, but
this time dealing them to only two discard
piles.
● For the second redeal, gather up the two
discard piles, but then deal to only one
discard pile.

Tips

Much of the skill in playing Three Pyramids
comes from planning which cards are to
remain within the main pyramid, and which
must be extracted, at various stages of the
game.

♣ VIRGINIA REEL

A variation on the 'building by numbers' theme, this time building by threes. This demanding game gets its name from the 'dance' of cards which takes place when some moves are made.

Cards

Two standard 52-card decks.

The layout

Place a 2, 3 and 4 of different suits face up in a column at the left. These are the first foundations. To the right of each card deal seven cards face up in a row. Deal a fourth row of eight cards face up below the first three rows. These cards start the reserve. Aces are dead cards and are discarded as soon as possible. (See sample layout overleaf.)

Aim

To move all the 2s into the top foundation row and build each one up in suit and by intervals of three to J: 2, 5, 8, J. Similarly, to move all the 3s into the middle foundation row and build these in suit by threes to Q: 3, 6, 9, Q. To arrange all the 4s in the lower foundation row and build these in suit by threes to K: 4, 7, 10, K.

A sample layout

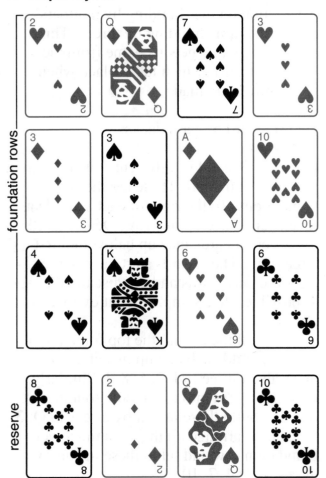

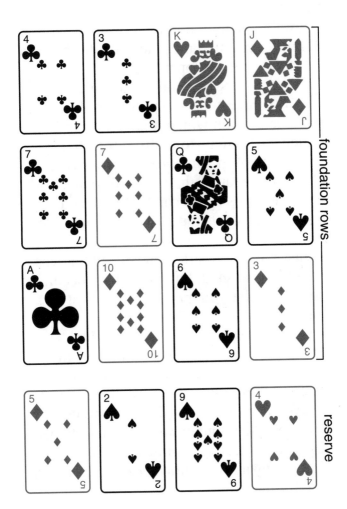

Playing

- Building is upon foundations only, and building can only take place on a foundation card that is in its proper row.
- The card to be built on a foundation must be of the same suit as, but three ranks higher than, the card on which it is built.
- Such a card may come from the bottom row or one of the three foundation rows.
- If from the latter, then the card may only be moved if its space can be filled by a 2, 3, or 4 (whichever is the required foundation for that row).
- This 'knock-on' effect means that moves are often restricted, but where they occur, they often affect more than one row at a time.
- Any potential foundation card which is present, but in its wrong row, may be moved to a gap in its foundation row, providing one exists and providing it too can be replaced by a foundation card of the appropriate rank.
- Aces in the foundation rows can only be discarded if they can immediately be replaced by a foundation card of the correct rank for that row.

● Additionally, any two or three foundation cards that are in the wrong rows may be swapped, providing the result is to bring them all into their correct rows.

● Aces are immediately discarded from the reserve and are not replaced until the next deal.

● When initial moves are exhausted, deal a further row of eight cards face up and overlapping the bottom (reserve) row, filling any spaces made by moving cards.

● Any aces that appear are discarded.

● Make whatever moves you can using the exposed cards of the bottom row.

● Whenever play comes to a standstill, deal another row of eight cards face up on the reserve piles.

● Continue playing and dealing in this way, until the stock is used up.

● There is no redeal.

Tips

Do not be in a rush to swap foundation cards between rows if this means that you will later cause a foundation card to become buried in the reserve. Leave your options open.

4.Games using two stripped decks

● SIXTY-FOUR SQUARE

A straightforward game which usually comes out. It needs a moderately large amount of space.

A sample layout

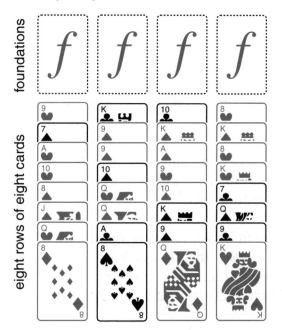

foundations

eight rows of eight cards

Cards

Two standard 52-card decks from which all
the 2s, 3s, 4s, 5s and 6s have been removed,
giving a Bezique pack of 64 cards.

The layout

Deal the cards face up in eight overlapping
rows of eight cards each, thus forming eight
columns. Aces, when released during play,
go in a foundation row above the layout.

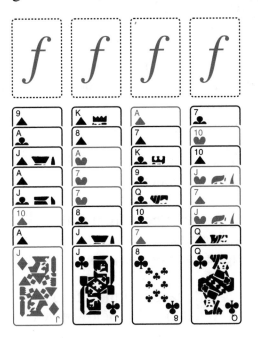

Aim

To build up the foundation aces in suit to Ks in the sequence: ace, 7, 8, 9, 10, J, Q, K.

Playing

● The exposed card of each column is available for play to foundations, building upwards within suit.

● Alternatively, it can be played to other exposed cards, building downwards in alternating colour.

● The removal of an exposed card releases the one below.

● A space made by clearing away an entire column is filled using any available card.

● There is no redeal.

● ZINGARA

A quick and easy game whose outcome depends largely on chance.

Cards

Two standard 52-card decks from which all the 2s, 3s, 4s, 5s and 6s have been removed, giving a Bezique pack of 64 cards.

The layout

Remove any 7 and place it at the left to start a row of eight foundation 7s. Below it deal

the cards, as they come, face up in an
overlapping column. When the next 7 is
turned up, place this to the right of the first
one, and then deal an overlapping column
below the new 7. Continue in this way,
forming a row of 7s with a column of
overlapping cards below each 7.

When an 8 turns up during the deal, you
may build this on an available 7 in the
foundation row, irrespective of suit. If a 9
then turns up, you may build this on the 8.
During the deal, you may build on any of
the foundation 7s, irrespective of suit, but
only as far as the 9. (See sample layout
overleaf.)

Aim

To build up the 7s to aces, turning the
corner, and regardless of suit.

Playing

● The deal complete, the exposed card of
each column is available for play to
foundations. There is no play to other cards
in the layout.

● A space made by clearing away a column
may be filled using the available card from
another column.

A sample layout for Zingara

foundations
row of 7s

columns

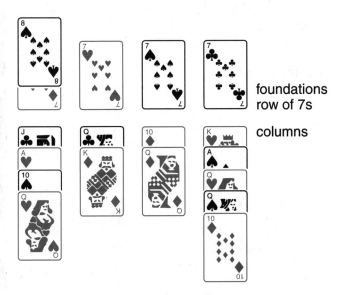

foundations
row of 7s

columns

◆ BOOMERANG

A straightforward game in which the
probability of winning or losing is about the
same. If the game is lost, the end comes
quickly.

Cards

Two standard 52-card decks from which all
the 2s, 3s, 4s, 5s and 6s have been removed,
giving a Bezique pack of 64 cards.

The layout

Deal three rows of four cards each, face up.
Four 7s, one of each suit, as they become
available go in a foundation row above the
layout.

A sample layout

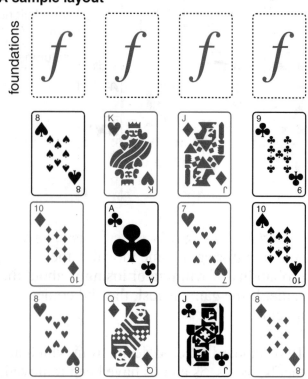

Aim

To build up the foundation 7s to aces and back again, within suit in the following sequence: 7, 8, 9, 10, J, Q, K, ace, K, Q, J, 10, 9, 8, 7, ace.

Playing

● An exposed card in the layout may be played to the foundations.

● Alternatively, it may be played to another exposed card, building up or down within suit, but not changing direction once a build is established.

● Within the layout, a K or a 7 may be built on an ace, but an ace built on a K terminates that ascending sequence.

● Where a space opens up in the layout, the space must be filled by a card dealt from stock.

● When moves are exhausted, turn up a new card from stock.

● If the new card cannot be placed, the game is lost.

1	2	3	4	5	6	7	8	9	10
11	12	13	14	15	16	17	18	19	20
21	22	23	24	25	26	27	28	29	30
31	32	33	34	35	36	37	38	39	40
41	42	43	44	45	46	47	48	49	50
51	52	53	54	55	56	57	58	59	60
61	62	63	64	65	66	67	68	69	70
71	72	73	74	75	76	77	78	79	80
81	82	83	84	85	86	87	88	89	90
91	92	93	94	95	96	97	98	99	100
101	102	103	104	105	106	107	108	109	110
111	112	113	114	115	116	117	118	119	120
121	122	123	124	125	126	127	128	129	130
131	132	133	134	135	136	137	138	139	140
141	142	143	144	145	146	147	148	149	150
151	152	153	154	155	156	157	158	159	160
161	162	163	164	165	166	167	168	169	170
171	172	173	174	175	176	177	178	179	180
181	182	183	184	185	186	187	188	189	190
191	192	193	194	195	196	197	198	199	200
201	202	203	204	205	206	207	208	209	210
211	212	213	214	215	216	217	218	219	220
221	222	223	224	225	226	227	228	229	230
231	232	233	234	235	236	237	238	239	240
241	242	243	244	245	246	247	248	249	250
251	252	253	254	255	256	257	258	259	260
261	262	263	264	265	266	267	268	269	270
271	272	273	274	275	276	277	278	279	280
281	282	283	284	285	286	287	288	289	290
291	292	293	294	295	296	297	298	299	300
301	302	303	304	305	306	307	308	309	310
311	312	313	314	315	316	317	318	319	320
321	322	323	324	325	326	327	328	329	330
					336	337	338	339	340
									350